Samuel Gordon

A handful of exotics

Scenes and Incidents chiefly of Russo-Jewish Life

Samuel Gordon

A handful of exotics

Scenes and Incidents chiefly of Russo-Jewish Life

ISBN/EAN: 9783337130336

Printed in Europe, USA, Canada, Australia, Japan

Cover: Foto ©ninafisch / pixelio.de

More available books at **www.hansebooks.com**

A
HANDFUL OF EXOTICS

SCENES AND INCIDENTS CHIEFLY OF RUSSO-JEWISH LIFE

BY

SAMUEL GORDON

METHUEN & CO.
36 ESSEX STREET, W.C.
LONDON
1897

PREFACE

THIS is an age of exploration for the ethnographer no less than for the geographer. We are intruding into the *penetralia* of unknown territories, we are making inroads into the mysteries, yet unsolved, of the thoughts, customs, and observances of alien races. The ethnographer's function is rendered more urgent by the duty he owes to the interests of the spirit of future inquiry; he must take an impress of individual peoples before the barriers of isolation, behind which they have preserved their individuality unimpaired, are broken down by the onward sweep of progress, the ultimate, if far-off, goal of which seems to be cosmopolitanism.

It would be ludicrous were I to put forward these few tales as even the slightest contribution to the science. And yet in no case, perhaps, is the necessity of such racial stereotyping greater than in that of the Russian Jew. In view of the various schemes to repatriate him in the land of his ancestors, where the absence of ukase, " Pales of Settlement," and other amenities of his present condition cannot but metamorphose him out of all recognition,—schemes which, whether from a political or economical standpoint, bid fair at no distant date to become a question of European importance,—it may not be out of place to make an attempt, however imperfect by comparison with more competent exponents, to delineate a few of the characteristics which have made him, if not a picturesque, at any rate an interesting figure in the background of modern history.

Despite, or perhaps because of, the numerous occasions which of late have brought the Russian Jew into an unenviable prominence, he has remained to the Western world only a shadowy reality, a myth and a mystery; he is still a hieroglyphic which has been but imperfectly deciphered. Some consider he has been wilfully and maliciously created for the express purpose of tarnishing the glories of our civilisation, by reminding us that mediæval intolerance is not yet a thing of the past. However that may be, I have in these slight sketches endeavoured to depict the Russian Jew in his native surroundings as a creature possessing "organs, dimensions, senses, affections, passions," and actuated in his dealings both with his brother in faith as well as with his Gentile neighbour by the same motives, good, bad, and indifferent, which actuate those of his fellow-beings to whom the Providence of history has been less of a stepmother. No attempt has been made, apart from an occasional hint, to draw fine shades of distinction as regards the character, language, locality, even creed, which differentiate the various sections composing an aggregate of five million human souls; there has been intended no tirade against an unfathomable policy of systematic and gratuitous cruelty which blindly defeats its own ends. I have merely attempted to show that the Russian Jew lives in a world of his own, a world having its lights and its shadows, and, despite its intrinsic incongruities, bearing in the humanity and divinity which is its motor force a wonderful resemblance to the world we inhabit ourselves.

The two stories of non-Jewish interest included in this little volume are perhaps an anomaly. But they may be justified as being faint side-lights illustrating the environments in which the Russian Jew moves, and as such, if on no other count, let them stand and take their chance with the rest.

LONDON, *September*, 1896.

CONTENTS

	PAGE
THE FOURTH DIMENSION	1
AN ALIEN IMMIGRANT	26
THE REDEMPTION OF THE SERPENT	60
THE MIGRATION OF SAINT SEBASTIAN	91
THE ASCENT INTO HEAVEN	125
OUT OF THE LAND OF BONDAGE	143
RABBI ELCHANAN'S QUEST	173
THE MORDECAI OF THE SERFS	210
"WHOSE JUDGMENT IS JUSTICE"	242
COSSACK AND CHORISTER	267

THE FOURTH DIMENSION

"THIS day I am become a happy man in Israel—blessed be the name of the Lord!" rose Tarphon's jubilant cry. The proof of his gladness lay in his face; but the cause of it lay in his arms—a huddled-up, swaddle-clothed heap of two-hour-old humanity. "It is a boy—that was bravely done of thee, Mirzah; now we shall have some one to say the Sanctification over us when we are dead."

"What ails thee, Tarphon?" said Mirzah, looking reproach with her big wan eyes, for she had not strength enough to lay it into her voice; "in the hour that new life is given us, to take the name of death into thy mouth? Thou knowest not what thou sayest in thy transport. Give me back the child before thou swallowest it with thine eyes."

"There, selfish one that thou art!" was

the good-humoured reply. "May I not hold him and touch him for a little while? Thou grudgest me the joy of fatherhood, perhaps, and yet it is the first time in the ten years of our wedlock that I have tasted it."

"Tarphon!" and the gathering tears in the big wan eyes said the rest.

"Foolish one, I was but jesting;" and Tarphon stroked the limp hand that was stretched out to meet his. "I am very well satisfied with thee; he shall be a great scholar, and his fame shall ring through the world—that pleases thee, see, thou smilest—and no less than two bullocks and ten sheep shall be eaten at his marriage feast. To be sure, I know not what I am saying—I will go forth and tell the news in the town and in the houses of our friends and kinsfolk. Nay, let me look at him again—I shall not do him mischief."

No wonder that Tarphon was a little delirious. He was a man who had been blessed with chattels of many sorts; he owned manservants and maidservants, and his flocks cropped his own pastures for many an acre round. And now God had set this coping-stone upon his fortunes, and Tarphon was but human and might be excused for not eyeing the event with stoic indifference. His excitement kept him on his legs till late in the afternoon, and when he came home he was very tired. "Not with the walking," he explained to Mirzah, "but with the load of good wishes I have brought for all the three of us." And then he sat down at the bedside and thought for a long time.

"What sayest thou, Mirzah? I hold it is but right I should make some offering to the congregation, so that the birth of Tarphon's son may be remembered for many ages to come."

"When I am recovered, I and my sisters shall embroider a covering-cloth for the Reader's pulpit," suggested Mirzah.

"It will get worn out in a few years," objected Tarphon, "and the gift is not one of sufficient value."

"Then let it be a golden wine-beaker."

"That might get stolen. Nay, do not prompt me; I have the gift in my mind. I have heard much talk to-day that Benish, the great scribe of Gostoneen, has finished the Scroll of the Law which he affirms to be the best handiwork of his lifetime, and he asks for it a large sum—I know not how much; but the harvest has been plentiful this year, and there has been no foot-rot among the sheep. I shall give what he asks—I shall not miss it."

So then, as proposed, Tarphon went to negotiate with Benish on the following morning; and when he entered, the expert was sitting in his scriptorium busily examining old parchments that needed repair.

"I have come about the scroll that I have heard say is the wonder of the world," began Tarphon.

"It is disposed of, or nearly so," answered Benish, "for the congregation of Wilna has offered me eleven hundred and fifty roubles for it."

"I will give you twelve hundred," said Tarphon.

"There is only one man can do that, and that is Tarphon of Stchelno."

"I am Tarphon, and yesterday a son was born to me; and I would present the scroll to the congregation in memory of it."

"The gift is worthy of the man and the occasion," said Benish; "you shall buy it. And now come and let me show it you."

And then from the inmost receptacle of his storing-place came forth the precious manuscript. It was of medium size and compact, nor yet so unwieldily bulky as many of the scrolls that weary the arms of the holders when they are carried about in procession on the Day of Rejoicing in the Law. And Benish's eyes glowed as he commented on its excellences.

"Ten years I have worked at it, and now every flourish is in its place, and the spacings and margins between the portions are measured to a hair. Look at the handles—solid ebony from the land of Kush, and the silk coverings at the back are such as the Indias cannot outvie."

And then he showed Tarphon the accoutrement and the accessories that belonged to the scroll; how the breastplate of solid silver was worked into the effigy of King Solomon's temple, with the peristyles and vestibules daintily fretted out from the bulk. And the large head-bells were the shapes of crowns, and the clappers inside gave out a sound like cymbals. As for the pointer, the upper part was in form of a palm branch tapering off into a delicately chiselled hand.

"And all these things were fashioned by my son, the silversmith," added Benish, proudly. "I tell you, no finer scroll exists—unless it be the one from which the patriarchs read the Sabbath-portion in the Garden of Eden; and it is yours at the twelve hundred and fifty roubles you named."

Tarphon stood gazing with open mouth at the splendours before him, and he had not the heart to haggle about the extra fifty wherewith Benish had saddled him; the man deserved his price.

And when Tarphon came home he told his wife: "I have beheld what no human eyes have seen; it was like drinking in the veritable glory of God."

"Nay, talk not so big," broke in Mirzah. "I, too, have been feasting mine eyes upon the shadow of the shadow thereof. But be still—he sleeps."

"The child—our child!" breathed Tarphon; and then he went on in a whisper, "What sayest thou to this, Mirzah: was it not at the hour of eight that he first drew breath? And Benish told me that was the instant when he put the last stroke to the writing of the scroll, having worked at it through the night into the morning; and so it might be said that they were born in the same winking of the eye. Is it not strange?"

"Strange?" said Mirzah. "Oh, thou niggard of faith! Is not God rich enough to dower the world with two blessings by one outstretching of the hand? Call it not strange; say rather it is a happy omen and foreshadowing that good fortune shall be his, having chanced upon such a co-eval."

Then Tarphon stooped over the child, and, kissing it, he whispered, "Dear as is to the Almighty His Law, so be thou, His creature."

But there were many things that demanded attention, and Tarphon had his hands full for the next five days that elapsed before the child might be initiated into the Covenant of Abraham. And the memory of that initiation-feast is still current through the country, for from the mere remains of it full two weddings might have been furnished forth. And for the occasion there had come all the men of consideration and importance in the neighbourhood; notably Rabbi Eliezar, the renowned Cabbalist, who it was said had once caught an angel by the foot and would not let him go until he had been promised a foremost place in the World-to-come. Now he was blind and palsy-stricken, and it was only a man of Tarphon's standing who might make bold to ask his company. And in the evening of the feast they brought the child, which had been named Ephraim, and laid it on the table before Rabbi Eliezar that he might give it his blessing; and he, alone of all the others, had been told of the wondrous coincidence that marked the finishing of the scroll and the birth of the child. And he laid his shrunken hand on little Ephraim's head, and, lifting his sightless eyes to heaven, he blessed him. Now the old man was toothless, and his utterance was vague and confused; but those who sat near him thought that these were the words he spoke:

"As ye are both cast within one nativity, so may its soul be also thy soul, and than the soul of the Word of God there is nothing purer and wholesomer on earth. But the Eternal breathed into the limitless vast, and they became, and were, the four things that are His dimensions. And as thou shalt abide by the blessings of the twin-soul that is thine, so shalt thou abide by whatever else may betide it; and as one shall be, so shall be the other. And if the twin-soul pass all the trials thereof, then shall it live appointed days."

And all who heard wondered what the blessing meant; but there was no one to give an explanation—not even Rabbi Eliezar, for he died on the way home from the feast of the Covenant.

The day following Ephraim's initiation was fixed for the Dedication of the Scroll; and in honour of this a general holiday prevailed through the town. Tarphon himself carried the scroll from his house to the synagogue in procession with the wardens and goodmen of the congregation. The House of Prayer was packed every inch, and from the galleries the women threw down cakes and sweetmeats, and there was great merriment and amicable strife in the catching of the dainties. But Tarphon's munificence was not yet at an end. In the opening paragraphs of Genesis, where the letters were only outlined, he chose the characters that made up the name of his son, "Ephraim ben Tarphon," to be filled in with ink; and the same he did with the last sentences of Deuteronomy, which had been left blank likewise. And for every letter he paid five roubles, all which went to the community to be given in charity to those that needed. Nor yet were the festivities done with, for on the thirtieth day from the birth took place Ephraim's redemption. And this means that he was repurchased from the priests of the town; for being a "first-born" he was, according to the Law, the due, and tithe, of the Cohanim, the descendants of Aaron. And Tarphon paid to every priest who asked for it the sum of ninety copecks, and again there was a plentiful feast provided. Occasionally Tarphon reflected on the strange blessing Rabbi Eliezar had uttered over Ephraim, but, though he knew a little more of the case, he saw therein no clearer significance than did the others; but it seemed to imply that an extraordinary destiny hung over his son that might turn to good or ill. Yet from the first Ephraim proved a source of joy. At the age of two he could say the alphabet from Aleph to Tov, and from Tov back to Aleph; and at three he boldly tackled the sesquipedalian monsters that are to be found in the "Sayings of the Fathers."

About this time Ephraim's career, which augured so well, almost came to an abrupt ending, and the thing was due to the carelessness of some one. For Mirzah had occasion to go upon some household errand, and had left the boy sleeping upon the couch, for the servants were about, and she knew he was safe. Now as to demons, burglars, and ravenous beasts he was certainly safe, for there were none in the neighbourhood. But in the very room where he slept there stood a monster made of glazed bricks that reached to the ceiling, and its inners were filled with burning embers. Now this monster-oven found that the flue through which it was wont to respire had become choked up, and the fumes which were to escape into the open were forced back into the cavity; and to obtain relief from the overcharge, the oven began to belch forth the noisome exhalations into the chamber, so that all the pure air became forced out through the crevices. And with the pain of the oppression, Ephraim awoke and started screaming with all the strength that yet remained in his poor tormented chest; and at that moment Mirzah rushed in and snatched him out of his peril just two heart-beats before it was too late. All the week he was sick and giddy, so that he was prevented from going to synagogue on the Sabbath with his father. And that was a sore disappointment to the little fellow. For he was now entrusted with the rolling-up of the swathe that served as a girdle for his scroll; and he was never happier than when at this task, although the stiff silken border proved a difficult matter for his little fingers. And that Sabbath there happened a strange thing in the synagogue. For while Naphtali, the master of the Cantilation, was reciting the weekly portion of the Law, he was seen suddenly to stop, and take off his spectacles; and then he rubbed his eyes and looked again. But though he rubbed spots out of his eyes, he could not rub the mistake from the page; for to be sure, the word for "breath," which ought to have been in the passage he had come up to, was missing from its place, and the sentence ran on mutilated and incoherent. And the wonder was how the deficiency had escaped notice so long, though at each reading the page had been closely scanned by three pairs of eyes—namely, those of Naphtali, who read, of the person who was called up to pronounce the blessing over the section, and of Tarphon who stood pointing. The next day Benish was summoned, and great was his consternation at the mishap.

"I don't know how this came about," he said in justification. "Every line I have gone over diligently after I had written it, and not even the tail of a Yod but was marked with unerring accuracy — but of this I can make nothing."

And then with dubious shakings of head he corrected the omission, and every one admired the skill wherewith he super-literated the erasure so that no trace of the tinkering remained. Tarphon was greatly grieved at the occurrence, for it jeopardised the reputation of the scroll. Still his grief was more than counterbalanced by the joy of Ephraim's speedy recovery.

And as the time went on Ephraim continued to make progress, so that at the age of seven he had already advanced to the study of Rashi and Onkelos and the commentators, and harassed his teachers with perplexing questions.

"Tell me," he once asked them, "if it happen that a man has searched every nook and corner of his abode upon the eve preceding the Passover, and has gathered all the crumbs and particles of leaven, so that nothing is left; but if during the festival a mouse should bring in from the adjoining dwelling, which is a Gentile's, a crust of bread and deposit it secretly in the Jewish house, is the owner thereof liable to the punishment of him who neglects the ordinance: 'Seven days there shall be no leaven found in your houses?'" And this, you must admit, is not a question which can be answered standing on one leg; and it was whispered that before every lesson his teachers held a conclave to be prepared with satisfactory answers to the precocious questioner. And Tarphon held his head high among the fathers of the congregation.

But little Ephraim was no mere bookworm; he romped about with the other children and excelled in their games. And thus it happened that a serious accident befell him. For one day, while playing at hare and hounds, he was chosen the hare; and seeing that one of his playmates had nearly come up to him, he looked about for a place of refuge or vantage. Now, in the corner of the courtyard where he had taken his flight there stood a large four-walled tank, rising to the height of three feet from the ground, that contained, as Ephraim thought in his perilous haste, dry fodder for the cattle; and if he could but attain that he was safe, for from there he could clamber over into the next courtyard, and his pursuer could not equal him in leaping. And at last he reached the side, and, vaulting over — splash! — down he went, for the tank was full of water and only sprinkled at the top with a thin layer of chaff; and once he sank, and twice, and at the third time a stableman had rushed to the spot, and barely reached him at the end of a pitchfork that caught in Ephraim's doublet. And so he was borne home a pitiable sight; his limbs stiff and his eyes staring wide; for the water he had swallowed had almost forced the life from his body. And when Mirzah saw him thus she set up a loud wailing, but

Tarphon only turned pale and helped her quickly strip him and put him into warm coverlets. By the Sabbath Ephraim had somewhat recovered, though he still remained a little ailing; and Tarphon went to synagogue to offer up thanksgiving for the sparing of his child. And the portion of the week was the crossing of the Red Sea; and when Naphtali had come to the passage where the waters parted, Tarphon suddenly clutched hold of his hand and bade him stop; for Tarphon's eyes had caught an error so glaring, that Naphtali might be pardoned for passing it without notice in the belief that his senses were playing him false. For the word "mayim," signifying "waters," was written such that the final "mem" bore the same shape as the initial "mem"; and the whole congregation came up one by one to examine the monstrosity of the thing, and certain remarks concerning Benish went from mouth to mouth that would not have pleased him. What? take such a treasury of money for work which a cobbler's boy would have performed more creditably? Such a thing had not been heard of ever since geese grew quills to make pens for scribes. And when Benish was called to see with his own eyes he stood tapping his forehead for a long time.

"Nay, my masters," he said at last; "this is not my handiwork. I am not a son of the soil, and I did not write this scroll in my sleep; but there is a mystery in this, I will swear that upon the scroll. There is an evil spirit lurking in the place; perhaps the man who blew the ram's horn on the First Day of the Year was unworthy of his office or incapable thereof, for he did not frighten the Satan away by the strength and excellence of his blowing, and that is the cause of this mischief." Many there were who believed the explanation and many there were who did not; and of the latter the most incredulous was Naphtali, for he himself was the man who had blown the ram's horn. And then Benish made the correction and went away; and when Tarphon came home he found Ephraim eating chicken-broth, and the flush of health had come back to his cheeks.

Ephraim continued to make good headway in all things. At the age of ten he began to keep all the fast-days, observing even the " Fast of the First-born " until the time of sunset; and he missed not a single service either in the early morning or in the evening of each day, and when his father was kept away by business he went by himself. And in all things relating to his religion he was most circumspect, and if the white of an egg showed but a tiny speck of blood he would not eat it, even though another were not immediately available. And yet for all this he did not seem to be spared trial and calamity. It was the time of counting the Omer, the seven weeks that elapse between Passover and Pentecost, when Ephraim had reached the age of eleven, that he went with the other children of the town to the river's bank, there to gather the youngling bulrushes which it is customary at this season of the year to strew across the floor, so that a pleasant savour might rise up from the sap. And Ephraim, in his eagerness to pluck only of the best, had strayed from his comrades, and did not notice how the soil was getting more and more porous and squelched beneath his footsteps. And suddenly it slipped away from him altogether, and there he was up to his waist in the slimy ooze; and, more by instinct than premeditation, he flung his arms aloft and grasped at the branches of the willow-tree that overhung his head, and that saved him. But it seemed to him that for the moment his arm must have lengthened to three times its usual measure, even as the arm of Pharaoh's daughter lengthened so that she might pull Moses from the water; for Ephraim could not understand how else he had reached the supports to which he clung. And there he might have remained during the night were it not for the poor washerwoman who plied her task a little further up; and when she had helped him out Ephraim enjoined her, giving her all his stock of savings, not to speak of his misadventure. And then he went home, very frightened, and changed his clothes before his parents might ask questions as to their condition. But what washerwoman ever recognised that she had a tongue to keep secrets with? And the tale of his son's escape soon reached Tarphon's ears, and at the news a thought flashed across his mind, undefined and vague, and he tried to connect its trail by dim links of memory with something else equally vague and undefined; but the more he followed it, the more subtly it escaped him. And again he renewed the attempt when it came about during the next reading of the Law, which took place on the second Sabbath of the Omer, that there was yet another alteration necessary in the scroll. For in the passage where it speaks of the houses of the lepers and of the mortar connected therewith, the word for mortar, which is "ongphar," and properly signifies "loam" or earth, was slightly shifted from its place, so that it stood slantingly below the level of the line. Now this was the eleventh time in eleven years that Tarphon had scanned the place, and never before had he remarked its peculiarity; and he knew it was no use sending for Benish to account for the thing, so on the day following he came and, without a word to any one, made the correction himself. But the event lay deeply in his mind, and he did not forget it for many a day.

At last came the time when Ephraim was to become a Son of the Commandments, and Tarphon determined that the occasion should be celebrated with befitting splendour. Of course Ephraim read before the congregation the whole portion of the week, and, in addition, the apocryphal chapter pertaining thereto; and that was a feat of which not everybody's son could boast. Not only that, but he delivered an oration of his own making, showing that he felt the responsibility of becoming a full-fledged member of the congregation; and the whole town was full of his praises, and Tarphon was vaunted indeed a man whose works turned out well. A month after Ephraim was to proceed to the great Talmud School of Vilosen, for he was to qualify for a Rabbi; but on the eve of his departure he complained of spots before his eyes, and there was a slight discoloration about his temples that became more and more apparent. This was his first serious illness, and Tarphon went betimes to change the boy's name, so that if it had been ordained—was not God's wisdom infinite?—that the Angel of Death should be deputed to lay his hand on him, Azrael might come and find some one who answered not to the name of him for whom he had been sent the errand. But despite of it Ephraim grew worse; a fever came over him, and the blood coursed seething-hot through his veins. Tarphon and Mirzah sat and looked at him, noting every breath he drew and every tremor of his body. And when Mirzah had fallen asleep with the weariness of the watching, Tarphon buried his head in his hands; but he did not weep—there was no time for that. He was busy tracing the flimsy thread of memory that he knew lurked somewhere in the recesses of his mind. And all at once a quaint phrase leapt forth therefrom, and he grew puzzled where he had heard it. "The four things that are His dimensions." That was something to work upon, and then came another recollection, which ran, "if the twin-soul pass all the trials thereof, then shall it live appointed days." Were not those the words which Rabbi Eliezar had uttered at Ephraim's initiation into the Covenant? And then Tarphon carefully pieced together his conjectures. In the week that Ephraim had nearly suffered death from the poisonous vapours, was there not missing from its place in the Scriptures the word "ruach," signifying the air, the clean breath of the nostrils? And then again, at the time when Ephraim was nearly drowned in the cattle tank, was not the word for "waters" found to be ill-conditioned—the end letter the same as the beginning, even as Ephraim had thought that the bottom of the tank was of like nature to the top? And Tarphon thought tremblingly of the last point: when Ephraim had gone to gather bulrushes, was there not an untoward dislocation of the word which means "earth," even as the ground had moved from its place under his feet? And so Ephraim had run the gauntlet of air, water, and earth, and in each case the scroll had suffered mishandling in the words of this meaning. And now it was clear to Tarphon that the "four dimensions of God" were, forsooth, the four elements, and the "twin-soul" was the spirit animating both his child and the scroll that had been born into life at one and the same moment. And what further proof did he need? Was not the boy writhing with the inflammation of his vitals? Was he not burning as with a fire? That was it—and Tarphon leapt up like a madman—there was some word signifying fire, flame, or burning which needed correction in the scroll, and if that were done the danger would be passed and the elements conquered, and his boy Ephraim would live long days and be a king among men. And so Tarphon stormed out through the door—he would search the scroll from beginning to end, even if the sight of his eyes perished over it. But suddenly he stopped—it was very strange: surely the sun had long gone down, and it was too early for the dawn; but over there to the west was a reddish glare that increased as he went on, and round the corner men came running, breathlessly shouting:

"Tarphon, Tarphon, the synagogue is in flames!"

And Tarphon dashed on with wolf-like eyes and gnashing teeth, and when he came up to the crowd that stood outside the burning edifice, he clove through them as a thunderbolt cleaves through ears of corn, shrieking: "The scroll, the scroll; or else he dies—he dies!" And before they could hold him he had rushed into the flaming chaos of destruction, tore down the aisle to the Sacred Ark that spat sheaves of fire at him—and lo, there was the scroll blazing like touchstone. But what of that? There was the scroll—in cinders or not, what mattered it? And out again he came, like a demon who has burst his chains, from amid the holocaust of his damnation. And on and on he ran, holding the charred trophy above his head—and when he came in they had just finished stretching the linen sheet over the starkening limbs and were turning the looking-glasses towards the wall.

Two days afterwards was the Fast of Ab, the anniversary of the destruction of Jerusalem, the day whereon are carried to the "Good Place" for burial all the torn leaflets and spoilt synagogue gear whereon appears the name of God; but the Scroll of Tarphon was buried in one and the same coffin with his son Ephraim. Say, are not these things wonderful?

AN ALIEN IMMIGRANT

If you prick us, do we not bleed?
Merchant of Venice.

HE—that is, Solomon—was certainly the oracle of the place. His authority on politics, art, science, and all other things that more or less affect this world and the next, was undisputed. Saturday, from midday to the hour of the afternoon service, he gave consultations, sat in his seat and uttered revelations. The family-heads who were *habitués* of the little place of worship listened to him open-mouthed and open-eared; but occasionally a casual visitor who knew not of Solomon's greatness would venture a suggestion, and then the floodgates of Solomon's wisdom were opened, and his knowledge came sweeping down in a torrent on the bold questionist, making sport of his opinion in a whirlpool of sense-bewildering information. I was perhaps the only one of his audience that knew what a humbug old Solomon was; I at least was aware that what the others thought the gleanings of a laboriously accumulated world-wisdom, was the spontaneous manufacture of the moment. Solomon had a vivid imagination : nothing else could account for the perversions of the natural order of things for which he was responsible—for the alliances between hostile dynasties, for translocations of vast territories, which gave the lie to all our received notions of geography—for regeneration schemes that would shortly make the earth a paradise. Still he was entertaining, and gave a distinct relish to the somnolent Sabbath afternoons that were apt to hang heavy on my hands. He was the beadle of the little congregation, and in his unconsecrated moments sold lottery tickets. In his after-business hours he wrote door-post amulets. He was also, for some mysterious reason, the best performer on the ram's-horn during the high festivals, and the fame of his efficiency brought him many pupils. Otherwise he was a solitary man, without kith or kin in London. Not that he seemed to want any one, because he managed very well for himself, bought his own provisions, kept his own house, which amounted to a single-roomed flat in Montague Buildings, and no one who looked at the squat, sturdy figure and the tawny beard would have credited them to a man of sixty.

I had seen Solomon pose as a demigod, and was very keen to know him as a man. Strong individuality was stamped like a hall-mark on every feature of his face, and made one forget its commonplaceness; and the expression upon it was one not acquired in the elementary school of tribulation. He seemed to have been taught one of those lessons which stock a man with sufficient education in character to last him all his lifetime. And if this was mere conjecture on my part, it was perhaps his habitual reticence about himself that made me drape his past with shadows. I did not, however, despair of solving this sexagenarian riddle.

One Sabbath afternoon I found him sitting in solitary grandeur. He explained to me that a domestic event had happened in the house of Stocklinski, the congregation treasurer, and that there had been an exodus *en masse* to 2, Penny Street, in token of goodwill to the new arrival and the two parties responsible for it. Solomon and the treasurer were eternally at feud, because the latter insisted on countersigning the receipts, which Solomon took for a slur on his trustworthiness. I blessed Stocklinski for his caligraphic officiousness, because it gave me at last an opportunity of a quiet *tête-à-tête* with Solomon.

"I am surprised to see how you bamboozle your seat-holders, Solomon," I said offhand; "if they found you out they would give you the sack."

He smiled all along the expanse of his strong, healthy teeth.

"The sheep's-heads," he said disdainfully in his peculiar idiom, half English, half everything else; "they know they have hands and feet, and nothing more, Isn't it the same all the world over? If you tell a lie and keep a sober face on it, not even Elijah the prophet would find you out—and this is not a congregation of prophets."

"Well, Solomon," I answered, "I am not much of a prophet myself, but I know when I get hoodwinked, and that ought to take the spice out of your fabrications."

"You misjudge me, my son, if you think I lie for the mere pleasure of lying," he said. "May there not be in a man's life one bitter truth, one sad reality, to forget which he dwells in a world of dreams and imaginings? And if he deceives others, he is perhaps but practising how best to deceive himself."

There was a pause; I felt the old man's rebuke, but I also felt that it contained no malice—only sorrow, infinite sorrow, such as my remark could not have caused were his nature the most sensitive.

"They say you were taken prisoner at Sebastopol——" I resumed.

"Quite true," he interrupted. "I came over as the Queen's guest—she sent me an invitation through thirty thousand men, several generals amongst them—and that is more than most foreigners over here can say." And he smiled at his own quaint view of the case.

My nerves began to tingle. Here was a man who had seen death and destruction in the wholesale, who had played skittles with his life and limb, and survived to tell the tale. I was young, and so I felt the strong fascination of the man who could talk so dispassionately of a reality, the mere conception of which set my flesh in a tremor.

"You were taken prisoner and conveyed to Plymouth," I continued, in order to keep the topic in evidence. Solomon had a habit of dodging the point at issue. "How does it feel to be taken prisoner in war?"

A far-away look had come into his eyes.

"Yes, I was brave in those days," he said slowly—"very brave; but then I did not care what happened, and perhaps it is an easy thing to be brave when you feel like that." He suddenly recollected himself, and went on with a short laugh: "Ah, you want to know how I was taken prisoner? Why, all the little children know the story; I have told it hundreds of times. Well, I was stationed in the south suburbs—Karabelnaya, I believe they call it; I don't know why, but the enemy seemed to be bearing us a special grudge, for it was here that their guns were closest to the city walls—ugly looking iron brutes with impudent prying nozzles.

Occasionally they suffered from a catarrh, and then they sneezed cannon-balls and coughed fire-clouds, till I thought it was Sodom and Gomorrah all over again, only that the righteous were no better off than the sinners. Every day the cursed things came nearer and nearer, till we scarcely had any breathing room left. I was serving in Poniatowski's regiment—a crew of dare-devils and scamps, who stole the boots from each other's feet and ate them. I tell you, leather was a delicacy in those days after the tallow had given out. The knife was grazing our throat, and Kerkoff, our colonel, went about like a dog with a scalded tail.

"'Children,' he said one day, 'do you see that powder-tower?'

"We saw it clearly enough; we were well acquainted with it for months. It was the enemy's chief ammunition depôt, and there were barrels and barrels of the deadly stuff in it.

"'Well,' Kerkoff went on, 'I want a man to make it jump; one man can do it, but he won't be much good for anything else afterwards. That will give us a respite before they bring up fresh supplies, and in the meantime perhaps we can break our way through. Who will volunteer?'

"Then we knew that one of us had to die. If there were no volunteers the lot would decide. So I stepped forward—I was afraid the lot would miss me."

"You, Solomon, volunteered?" I interrupted him with a start. "And for certain death, too? What made you do it?"

"What made me do it?" he repeated. I was used to his repeating my questions; it was not the effect of a laborious comprehension, but of the mechanical habit to which all that section of his race are subject. "I had nothing to live for—the bullets avoided me, though they slew right and left; and when you get tired of waiting for a thing, you go forth to meet it." He broke off, and again the far-away look came into his eyes.

I pitied him in silence; I could not do more—it is presumption to comfort a man if he chooses to make the shadows of his sorrow inscrutable.

"And yet you escaped?" I said, to arouse him from his reverie. "How did it happen?"

"How it happened?" he iterated, looking up heavily. "I have forgotten how exactly. I am an old man, and it is long ago; but I remember crawling through the trenches, fuse and tinder-box in hand, till suddenly I felt a grip on my shoulder and saw a young English officer—big as Og, King of Bashan—loom down upon me.

"'What are you doing here?' he said in Russian. I could not answer because his hold on me was so tight, so I showed him my fuse and the fire apparatus, and pointed to the powder-tower.

"'Oh, I see,' he gasped, and his teeth came together with a snap. 'Blow us up, did you want to? Well, you are an ambitious man, but your life before ours,' and he pulled out his revolver. 'However, I give you a chance—will you die, or surrender?'

"And as he was standing there, the long rod of his revolver bearing on me, I was reminded of Rabbi Nathan at the Talmud School—how he once stood over me with his cane because I did not know my lesson, and the lesson was a sentence from Mishnah: 'If a man consent to his own death, unless it be for the honour of God and our Sacred Writ, it shall be as though he were the cause thereof, and his blood shall be on his own head.' And the punishment of the suicide, you know, is Gehennah—you jump from the roaring furnace into the ice-cold water, and back again, and so on for all eternity. But that did not matter; I had got used to Gehennah and things worse in the last three months of the siege—what with scorching my skin brown in putting out the blazing buildings, and then shivering with ague during nights of sentry duty. And it all passed through my mind like a flash.

"'Then I will die, your honour,' I said. The officer looked startled.

"'Well, you are the first man who asked me to have his brains blown out,' he said; 'if I had liked the job I would not have given you a chance of asking. Anyway, I am not going to turn assassin to please a Russian, even if he is as brave as you are.

"'But I am a Jew, your honour,' I tempted him.

"He laughed. 'That makes no difference in our notions. I shall say that you have deserted, and then you won't get shot.' Then he called the guard. Well, you know the rest."

I was hanging spellbound on Solomon's lips. His narrative was like a rocket that has burnt itself to ashes before one could gather all its wonderful effects. The vacuum it left on my understanding was almost painful. And yet I comprehended the pregnant terseness, the absence of adorning, self-laudatory detail in the old man's simple words. It was that his adventure, apart from the distance of its occurrence and the familiarity of its recollection, meant nothing to him. It existed in his mind not for itself, but because it was the result of some cause, and the cause overshadowed the result and effaced it. It is not often that people give such an earnest of their satiety of life as Solomon had done.

"Yes, Solomon, everybody has his troubles," I remarked, more in answer to my own thoughts, and feeling half-ashamed of my platitude. "The difference is in the way we bear them: on some of us the least trifles fall like a sledge-hammer blow

—to others the heaviest tribulation is but a soap-bubble of fate."

"Do not our sages say the human heart is less brittle than iron?" he replied, with rather more interest than my truisms warranted. "I could tell you a story of a man——" he stopped, and looked at the round-faced clock that gave the little balcony connecting the two women's galleries quite a cyclopean appearance: "the masters will not be back for an hour—if you would care to listen to an old gabbler like me, I will tell you about something that happened years and years ago in my native country."

I nodded, because I would not let my eagerness betray me by my words; true I should have preferred hearing his own story, but I had a vague hope he would speak of something nearest his heart, and I should catch a glimpse of his calamity through the chinks of his parable.

"His father was the richest man in Kadaan," Solomon began without ado; "he kept a drink-shop, and as it stood a few hundred yards away from the village out upon the open road, it was the nearest to the farmers and the dealers coming from up-country to the market-town beyond, and the last on their return way till they again reached Trenka, which is the village before Kadaan; and this circumstance had a great influence on the custom of the tavern. Favish, the son—the man of whom I am telling you—served at the bar, but he did not like the occupation. The strange, bold faces he saw across the counter frightened him. He was much more comfortable in his little garret, trying to blow its roof off with his cornet. When he was a boy of twelve, his uncle had brought him a little tin trumpet, and that determined his vocation in life—a klesmer, a musician, he would be, and nothing else. By the time he left boyhood he was already an expert, and in great demand at all the festivities in the neighbourhood. By now he was quite a man, as reserved as ever, seeking his own company, plain-featured and clumsy, but ready to give his heart's blood for those he loved.

"One day Chananya, the glazier-huckster from Uldrodno,—who, by the way, was also district scavenger, because he picked up everything nobody else would lay hands on—came to Favish's father.

"'Mendel,' he said, with his wheezy chuckle, 'your son—may he live to be a hundred—is nearly four and twenty. It is time he had his own home and hearth, like a good Yehudi.'

"'Well, that has nothing to do with you,' said Mendel, gruffly. He did not like holding a long conversation with Chananya—it was almost a degradation for a respectable householder to speak to him.

"'Why not?' asked the other; 'he must marry, for the glory of the congregation—and besides, I have found him a bride.'

"'And who is she?' asked Mendel, smiling in spite of himself at the absurd idea.

"'My daughter,' answered Chananya, hardily, "as fine and respectable a girl as——'

"But here Mendel flew in a terrible rage.

"'What! you old carrion-flayer, you with your half-bred hussy of a daughter, you want to get hold of my Favish? Some evil spirit has driven you out of your senses—go home and pray God that you may be restored—my son for your daughter!'

"'And why not?' persisted Chananya; 'my daughter is good and respectable.'

"'Good and respectable!' shouted Mendel; 'what do people say of her—how many times has she run away from you?'

"'She was starving with hunger and cold, and when I came home and brought no money she went away, because we could not bear to look upon each other's misery,' said Chananya, whiningly yet glibly.

"'And where did she go to when she went away?' jeered Mendel.

"'I don't know,' said Chananya, 'but the spirit of the Lord is on all her ways.'

"'Then may the spirit of the Lord be a thousand miles hence,' cried Mendel, rendered profane by his exasperation.

"'Well, we shall see, Mendel—we shall see,' said Chananya, quietly, as he lifted his satchel and hobbled off.

"And the old schemer knew what he was saying. About a week afterwards, towards afternoon time, when the tavern was most crowded and Favish had to help at the bar, Chananya came in—and not alone. He brought his daughter with him; she was holding him up by the arm, because he pretended to have fallen lame, and that was his excuse for taking the girl with him on his rounds. And what a strange pair they made! No one would have guessed that they were trunk and branch: she, lissome as a withe and fresh as a myrtle; he, gnarled and bent and shrunken like a sapless bramble-stock. And then their faces—one was tempted to gaze long at the distorted grimace of the old man, to give oneself the luxury of the contrast. For Yenta's face was like a summer storm, terrible in its beauty. The hair was massed and black as the thunder-clouds, and her eyes could flash and strike hard as the lightning, and between the two arched the broad serene brow like the calm of the rainbow. And as she tripped in, modestly and demurely, trim in her ankle-long frock and neat apron, stepping daintily on the high-heeled morocco slippers, Mendel turned white to the tip of his nose, and cast an anxious sidelong glance at Favish.

"'A glass of vodka—of your best,' said Chananya, throwing a silver rouble on the counter. Mendel obeyed without a word, and Chananya stood there, with his daughter beside him, leisurely sipping his beverage instead of tossing it down as usual, for he could toss vodka with the best of them. Mendel kept furtively watching Favish; the young man looked terribly disconcerted, his hands seemed to be refusing him service, for he dropped two glasses, and spilt half a gallon of fire-wine. And all the while Chananya stood sipping, fully conscious that every eye in the room was fixed on him and his daughter.

"'Make haste, Chananya,' Mendel burst out at last, half-mad with anxiety; 'don't you see you take up the room of the other customers?'

"'What of that?' answered Chananya, looking him full in the face; 'have I not paid my money like the others, and have I not the right to drink my purchase fast or slow as pleases me?'

"'Well said, Melchizedek, or whatever your name is,' broke in Christopher Talka. He was the tallest man in the room, with a big red beard, and by trade he was a swine-dealer. 'Let the old man alone, Mendel; he can stay as long as he likes,' he continued, turning to the host. But everybody knew what Christopher meant—it was Yenta, not her father, whom he defended. Many a time he had kicked and hustled some way-worn pedlar out of the room with the words: 'Go and make hay for your cow and calves at home, and leave drinking to your betters.'

"'Let us go, father,' said Yenta, gently, while shooting a quick glance at Christopher; 'do not let us be the cause of quarrel—if these men are inhospitable, God will provide us other shelter.'

"Chananya turned grumblingly; he knew he was the hero of the hour, and he wanted to enjoy his triumph over Mendel a little longer. But still, Favish had seen Yenta, and that was the principal thing. So they went away, and all across the courtyard Favish's eyes followed them; but at the corner Yenta turned and smiled at him—yes, unmistakably at him. Then they disappeared, and Favish thought that the dark had set in early that day, and his legs tottered under him as if all the sinews had snapped.

"That is how the mischief began. From that day Favish was a changed man, and his father looked upon him sorrowfully, for he divined the reason of Favish's pale cheeks, and he cursed Chananya from top to toe for the evil he had brought on his boy. For Favish neither ate nor slept, but all day long he loitered about the high-road looking towards Uldrodno, as though he were expecting some one to come from there. At first he still toyed a little with his cornet, but that ceased too, and the house lay desolate with the silent misery of its two occupants; for it was two years now since Chavah, the faithful wife and mother, had been carried out of it, feet foremost. For several weeks things went on thus, while Favish was wasting to a skeleton; but still Mendel said nothing, because he thought the evil would die of the disease of time.

"But Favish came to him one day, laid his head on his father's shoulder, and burst into tears.

"'Send for her, father, if thou wouldst have me live,' he sobbed. 'I have tried, but I can no more—send for her.'

"Mendel waited till he had gulped down his own tears. 'Son, dear son,' he said at last, 'conquer thyself. She is not for such as thou art; she will not make thee a good wife. Let her go her own way, and do thou go thine.'

"'I cannot, father,' whispered Favish; 'she haunts me; her face mocks me for my impotence when I endeavour to forget. Oh! I am so helpless, and the ache in my heart is killing me. Thou canst help me, father—help me!'

"'I should be helping thee to thy own destruction,' said Mendel, despairingly.

"'I must have her, father, if it be for my destruction in this world and the next,' cried Favish. 'I have lost my health, my skill, everything that made life pleasant to me. Yesterday I tried to play my sorrow away, to be David to my own Saul, but an iron grip held me by the throat and choked my breath. And so it will be as long as I live—help me, father!'

"'If it must be, Favish,' said Mendel, tremblingly, 'then let it be in God's name. I will not see thee despair if thou hast made me thy hope. Besides, shall I play Providence to any man?'

"At these words Favish started up with a cry of joy, seized his father's hands, and kissed them again and again. Then it was settled that Mendel should go to Chananya on the morrow and talk things over. What passed between them and what terms and conditions of marriage they arrived at Favish never knew, nor did he care in the fulness of his joy. The face of Mendel, when he returned with the news of Chananya's approval, was not that of a messenger of glad tidings; the furrows in his forehead had deepened, and his hair was perhaps a tinge whiter. But Favish saw nothing, and the first time he held Yenta in his arms he felt a giant's strength come over him, and was certain that no human evils could make part of his fate.

"The news of the marriage created a great stir in the neighbourhood; and when the first wave of astonishment had settled down, every now and then another gossip came, shaking his head and talking under his breath to Mendel. And the usual conclusion to what they had to tell was, 'Do not take it ill, Mendel; I speak to you as a friend.'

"To one and all of them Mendel listened quietly, and at the end he replied,

'I will not believe anything. My son loves her, and soon she will be as flesh of my flesh. For the honour of my son, and for my own honour, I will not believe anything to her shame; and now go in peace.'

"And whether Mendel's rebuke offended them, or whether there was some other reason, few of his friends attended the wedding, and on Chananya's side not so much as a dog turned up to do him honour in his hour of joy. But guests or no guests, Yenta was Favish's wife irrevocably, and the weal and woe of one was the weal and woe of the other.

"For some time it seemed as though the raven-croak of the gossips and Mendel's misgivings were doomed to disappointment. Yenta was a model housewife, and her husband did not find her wanting in the matter of wifely affection. Old Chananya kept himself scarce, and on the rare occasions when he came to the hostel he was quite respectable. They had found him a decent lodging, and as he had no longer need to beg or to perform antics in the huts of wood-choppers and glass-blowers—for he had been a clown in his younger days—in return for a night's shelter, he had managed to acquire some self-respect. True, it sat on him like an ill-fitting secondhand coat, but it was there. Favish was in high spirits. He improved wonderfully in his art now that he had somebody besides himself to work for; and in the meantime the business of the tavern prospered and throve, for the fame of the beautiful hostess spread over the country around, and a good many did not mind going a little out of their way to get a glimpse of her. Old Mendel went about in a dream and held his breath, for fear of an evil eye.

"It was about a year after the marriage that first a strange thing happened. Mendel and Favish had gone over to Trenka to see about a new supply of drink-stuff for the shop. They made their bargain, and returning, had found a lift on a corn-waggon, which brought them home an hour earlier. And as they entered the courtyard they saw, sitting at one table, Yenta and Christopher Talka, the swine-dealer; and as neither of them was deaf, there was no need for them to have their heads so close together. Two full glasses were on the table, and Yenta was spreading a pack of cards one by one.

"Favish gave a gasp and stood still at the door, and Talka scrambled hastily to his feet, almost upsetting the table in extricating his long legs. Yenta kept a smiling countenance.

"'Talka asked me to tell him his fortune,' she said, looking at Favish without wincing. Favish answered not a word, but passed on into the stables. Mendel's, however, was the wisdom of maturer years; he saw it was a case where silence would speak the loudest, so, despite the quaking of his heart, he forced a jest to his lips.

"'What! a big fellow like you, Christopher, afraid of a hare that has run across your path?'

"Talka twisted and turned awkwardly from side to side.

"'Mere pastime,' he mumbled, 'mere pastime;' and with a sheepish laugh he edged out by the door.

"All during the rest of the day father and son avoided each other. Perhaps they were afraid of reading the confirmation of some nameless dread in each other's face. Yenta went about her duties unconcernedly; she seemed ignorant that anything uncommon had happened, and Favish did not tell her.

"But she soon made it apparent that things were not with her as they had been; she became peevish and uneven in her temper, and her husband did not always know what answer he might expect. Sometimes she was moody and thoughtful, and at others uproariously merry. But her laugh was not pleasant to hear; it was loud and strident, almost like a shriek, and occasioned by things that ought to have made her blush in her husband's presence. For she busied herself more and more with the customers, and took a great interest in their affairs. So the reserve which her prim, quiet demeanour had at first kept up began to wear off, and the fault was none but hers. Was it seemly that she should stand leaning on both elbows across the counter, drinking with the peasants, and mixing in their talk? And if now and then one caught her by the hand, she did not draw it away in anger, as a well-behaved matron should have done Talka was invisible for a month or so; then he started coming again, at first rarely, then more often, till that flaring red beard of his was the most familiar sight in the public room. Chananya, too, became a more frequent visitor, and each time he brought a new rent in his coat and a more unquenchable thirst. There he would sit, with a besotted look in his eyes, till he was drunk, and then he got on the table, the empty bottle in hand, and danced the Cossack dance; and Yenta's laughter rang louder than all the others', louder even than Talka's. Mendel turned white as death, and Favish said nothing, but went out into the stables. More and more the control of things passed out of their hands. Yenta did all the business, kept the accounts and the money, and doled it out to them grudgingly, as one does to strangers.

"'Make an end of it, Favish,' said Mendel one day, brokenly. 'Tell her that Chananya and—and the swine-dealer must not come to the house any more, or I shall not survive it.'

"'Yes, father,' answered Favish, looking away; 'I shall tell her—I shall tell her of it to-morrow.' And to-morrow came, and still he did not tell her; and again it was to-morrow, and always to-morrow. For whenever he looked at his wife his accursed love for her mastered him and held him tongue-tied. And so Talka flaunted his red beard more overbearingly than ever, and Chananya drank and drank till he fell under the table or wallowed in the passage snoring off his drunkenness, while the peasants kicked and trod and spat upon him as they passed in and out. And Yenta saw it and laughed. Mendel saw it too, but with failing eyes, and perhaps he would have cried were not his heart beating too faintly to stir him to tears. And one morning it had ceased to beat altogether. Favish raved with grief; yet through it all, strange to say, a vague feeling of relief came over him. He was alone now—there was nobody standing by to count every leap and quiver of his heart; and his pain was less, because it was not doubled by agonising that other loving breast. And at least he was now secured against that terrible 'Make an end of it, Favish,' for the loving tongue that had uttered it was now silent for ever. Favish was very patient; he had faith in the goodness and fitness of things, and the day would arrive when Yenta would come to him unasked, and bring him the love a wife should bring her husband.

"And so he waited, and for a whole year nothing happened, except that Yenta's face more and more often wore a red flush, and that she became a great expert in all games of cards. Talka went in and out as usual, and brought her mysterious packets, the contents of which Favish was never told. The only important event before things came to a finish was that Chananya was found one day at the bottom of a fox-pit with his neck broken. And that was the end of Chananya. Yenta did not trouble to observe the week of mourning.

"It was the Sabbath after Chananya's funeral. For the first time since many months Yenta had stood by to hold the candle while Favish was saying the Sabbath-eve blessings on the ensuing week; and afterwards she had gone up to him and had stooped—for she was much taller than he—to kiss him. Favish did not know what was happening, and as he went up to his room to fetch his cornet, he had to grope his way, for the tears of happiness were blinding him. At last it had come, all that for which he had hoped and waited and suffered. That night he had to go to Trenka to play at a wedding feast; for, as is usual in that part of the country, the marriage had taken place on the Friday, and the feast was left for the following Sabbath evening. Favish cursed his fate at having to leave home, but he had promised. And as he walked along the road, all ablaze with the silver of the full moon, he was almost glad to be alone with his happy thoughts. Half-way along he heard cries, and the trampling of beasts, and when they came nearer he saw it was Talka driving with voice and whip a herd of swine in close tether. As he saw Favish, he became quiet, and tried to hasten the beasts by a shower of blows.

"'Where are you going, Talka?' asked Favish, with a sudden dread shooting through him.

"'I must hasten on to Slonim,' answered Talka. 'I want to get there by midnight, so as to give my beasts a rest, and make them look fit for to-morrow's market—we have already come a long way.'

"Favish looked at him; but Talka seemed speaking the truth: his face was red and heated, and the hoofs of the swine were trodden to the blood, for a red trail stretched in the direction from which they came.

"Favish reached Trenka in another hour; and when he came there, there was to be no wedding feast after all; either the cook had let the dishes burn, or the bridegroom had run away overnight—something had happened to stop the proceedings. Favish was very pleased; he saw in it a good sign, and he turned back without a word of chiding for having been made to come a fool's errand. The ground flew under his feet, for his heart was light and his step was light, and before he knew it he saw the palisade fence that hedged the tavern on one side gleam white in the distance. And as he came nearer, he heard voices floating through the still summer night—voices that he knew, for at the sound a leaden weight hung itself upon his feet, and, dropping on his hands, he crawled to the edge of the enclosure.

At the gate stood Yenta, with her thick hair falling like a mantle around her shoulders, and one of her hands in Talka's; the herd of swine lay around them in dead weariness.

"'And so it will be to-morrow?' Talka was saying, gazing in Yenta's eyes; 'thou hast kept me long enough.'

"'I could not come before this, Christopher,' replied Yenta. 'There was father—after all he was my father, and if I went away he would be cast out upon the streets, and I could not let that be done.'

"'Very well, sweetheart, so be it then,' said Talka, 'I shall come to-morrow night and take thee away; and listen, dear, get ready whatever there is, the roubles and that gold beaker and the silver candlesticks—the broad-nosed Jew, what does he want them for?—and then we shall go far away, to my home in Croatia, and thou shalt eat swine flesh to thy heart's content. Didst thou like the bacon I brought thee?'

"'I liked it, but I like thy kisses better, Christopher,' she said. 'I tried to kiss him to-night, in order to allay his suspicions, and I have a taste on my lips as if I had been eating crab apples—kiss me hard, Christopher,' and she stretched out her mouth to meet his.

"Favish listened and looked; then life came back to his limbs—if his ears had been dishonoured, his eyes were not to be dishonoured too; and so, quick as lightning, he snatched up his cornet, set it to his mouth and blew. And he blew as no man on earth had done before or will do after him; and perhaps the sound of the trump of judgment will ring out like that. At first it was like the whining of a wolf's cub, then it swelled like the distant thunder on the hills, and at last it rose like the shriek of Satan when he tried to force his way into Paradise and got his knee jammed in the gateway. At the sound Talka started up with a yell, and ran— and ran as fast as he could waddle on his fat haunches. And, despite everything, Favish had to throw down his cornet and to lean against the fence, for the maniac laughter that shook him threatened to burst his sides. Then he strode towards Yenta. She had been standing there, white and moveless as a pillar of salt; and just near her Favish saw something glittering on the ground—it was Talka's butcher-knife, which he had dropped as he scampered off; it was long and turned up to a point at the end like his own impudent nose; nor was it straight and square like those which our licensed slaughterers use. Favish picked it up and stood before his wife.

"'So thou eatest the flesh of swine?' he asked.

"She looked at him, but even her eyes had lost their power of speech.

"'Then I shall give thee a feast, such as thou never hadst in all thy days,' he screamed, and threw himself on the herd of swine and hacked and slashed and sliced among them—wherever his knife plunged; and he shrieked with laughter to see the quivering carcases and the helpless struggles of those that survived to break away from the tether. And each time he struck a more murderous bow, or made a more deadly gash, he cried, 'So much for thee, friend Talka.' Now and then he looked round to see whether Yenta was standing where he had left her. And when he had finished, he went up to her, twined his hand in her hair, and dragged her along towards the slaughtered swine.

"'Eat, eat,' he shouted, 'there is enough and to spare,' and with one push he sent her staggering on to the heaving, tossing flesh-mountain. Then without another look or word, he went out into the night."

. . . .

Solomon ceased, and his head fell heavily on his breast. I dared not look at him.

"And what became of Favish?" I whispered.

"What became of Favish?" he repeated. "He exchanged with a conscript, went to the war, and was taken prisoner in the trenches of Sebastopol trying to blow up the English powder magazine."

THE REDEMPTION OF THE SERPENT

> Not the generous fool who his gift bestows
>   Since he cannot answer nay,
> Who opens his hand and laughs and goes
>   His old unconscious way,
> But the man who knows the full worth of his gift
>   And gives, tho' he gives with a frown—
> For he gives with his dole a share of his soul—
>   'Tis he deserves the crown!
>   *Saying from the Ramban* (spurious).

"NAY, Bylah, let not that be your last word. Can I say nought to soften your heart?" And the man, as he spoke, looked piteously at the girl.

"Importunate that you are," she answered, impatiently; "if my answer pains you, what profits it you to make me repeat it? It cannot be, Gedaliah—let the thought go from your mind."

"And why can it not be?" he persisted.

"Because—because people say you are not a good man, that you smoke on the Sabbath, and game and drink."

He hung his head. "But you can make me good," he said at last.

"I?" she asked. "God forbid that I should take such a task upon me—I that am ignorant in all but what pertains to a woman's knowledge; I can repair a tattered frock to look like new, but——"

"But a tattered soul like mine is beyond mending, you would say," he broke in bitterly.

"Nay, I said not that," was the quick reply. "To every man it is given to conquer the evil mind that leads him to transgression; go frequently to the House of Prayer, give unto the poor with open hand, and seek the company of godly men. Many have found deliverance in this wise."

"And when I have done so, what as to the marriage?"

"That can never be," she said, resolutely. "I love you not."

He drew a deep breath—it was scarcely a sigh; whoever heard Gedaliah sigh?

"If not, then not," he said, with philosophic shrugging of shoulders; and then he turned on his heel and went.

There were other reasons that prompted Bylah in her reply. For instance, Gedaliah was a Littvak; and it is well known that every self-respecting Pollak spends all his hours of leisure and all the time he plays truant from his business in thinking small beer of his Lithuanian coreligionist, though his ancestors may have been Gaonim and Talmud-diplomés for four generations. Furthermore Gedaliah walked a little stiff in his right leg, the result of a gunshot in the calf. That meant, of course, that he had been a frontier smuggler, and had helped to carry contraband bales of tobacco and tallow, for which a patriotic Government sentry had felt himself called upon to remind him, by a badly-aimed bullet, that the Holy Russian Empire was not to be trifled with, and required an unusual amount of caution and great swiftness of limb before it might be circumvented. The calling of contrabandist is not of an edifying nature, nor are its professors, as a rule, desirable acquaintances; but it is lucrative, and those who manage to escape

REDEMPTION OF THE SERPENT 63

the official remuneration in lead, have usually made good provision for an unauthorised payment in more precious metal. Gedaliah must have been lucky in his enterprises, apart from the above-mentioned misadventure; for he was well off, although he drew his income from no apparent sources. But Bylah did not tell him that her chief motive for rejecting him lay not in unorthodox habits, nor in differences of dialect, nor in stray excise-ammunition. What had it to do with him or anybody else, that there was a certain understanding between herself and one called Aryah, by profession a leather-hawker? They had arrived at it without outside interference, there had been no ceremonious go-between, no contracting middleman. They knew each other, and loved each other, and that was all; and despite the anomaly of the case, they were happy none the less. The cause for this directness in the hymeneal negotiations was to be found in the fact that they were both in reduced circumstances as regards the possession of parents. Aryah had owned to the deficiency unblushingly since the days of his boyhood; and

Bylah had made shift with the person of a maternal grandmother, who, however, by reason of the infirmities of age, had long thrown the responsibility of Bylah's existence on to her own shoulders. And now they were waiting till Aryah had talked the neighbouring peasantry into the belief that the quality of his leather was unexampled since the creation of cows and other dermatophorous quadrupeds; for naturally, upon this belief depended the profits of his business, and consequently the consummation of his promise to Bylah.

And at last they thought they could venture upon it. The wedding was an unpretentious affair, just serving its purpose and nothing more. There was no honeymoon; people of their standing believe in commencing the book of matrimonial life without reading the poetic dedication; they get on to the prose of it at once. And so it was with Bylah and Aryah. On the morning following the marriage, Aryah slung his bag across his shoulder and started on his professional tramp as usual, but, if anything, he was a little keener in driving his bargains. Bylah went about her household duties with a happy little smile, for she was conscious that on her rested the sentiment of the transaction. And therefore she did not forget the practical part of it. She went to the butcher and felt that she had a substantial interest in life; and as she sat peeling her potatoes she became aware that she was doing and managing for an eminently rational purpose. It was a change from the eternal gruel and meal-soup of grandmother's diet, ever since the old lady lost all her teeth and most of her senses. And as she watched the bubbling saucepan, Bylah remembered with gladness that somewhere upon earth there was a set of strong, healthy mandibles and a well-ordered digestion, the owner of which belonged to her; and the sense of ownership was grateful to the lonely soul that had gone its way in solitude where the milestones were so far apart, and one so very like the other. What it was she knew not, but the world seemed to have narrowed wonderfully in its compass. And so she determined that, come what may, she would try to deserve her good fortune, that she would be a helpmeet to her husband, and take upon herself their sorrows and leave for his portion their blessings. Such were her thoughts; but is it not a little sad when happiness may not be its own excuse?

Every evening she went beyond the village in the direction from which he was coming.

"Let me carry the wallet, crown of my soul," she would say, wiping the sweat from his face.

"Nay, life of my heart," would be the answer, "I am not tired; I sat and rested awhile on my way. What wouldst thou think to see me coming along on tottering limbs and with straitened breath? 'I have married an old man,' thou wouldst think. And is it not better I should leave my weariness among the stones of the wayside than bring it as far as thy arms?"

"But the burden is heavy——"

"Not so heavy as when I bore it forth in the morning," smiled Aryah; "if it were, what would become of us?" And then out came the pieces of silver and now and then a paper rouble; and Bylah felt it was good to live, and that love was the true service of Heaven, for which they were blessed as recompense with sufficiency of sustenance; for poverty is the mother of strife and discord.

Such was the routine of their life. But for them it held no monotony; there was always something new. Day by day they discovered in each other some undreamed-of excellence, and rivalled each other in the display of loving forethought. In the evening Aryah chopped the firewood for the coming day, and fetched the water from the pump; and Bylah was up with the sun to prepare the hot foot-bath that would alleviate for Aryah the hardships of the day's travelling. But of all days they preferred the Sabbath; for then, of course, Aryah did no business, and they were together from morn to night. And as he sat at the midday table and looked around him, Aryah's face gleamed with pride. Was he not now a "master of the house," of a rank with the other men of the congregation, though they had beards reaching to their girdles? And at his side sat she, who was at once his domain and his despot, his vassal and his queen—Bylah, gentle, patient, ready to shed for him her heart's blood; he felt that was the truth, and a man who feels that even once only in a lifetime has justified his existence. And when the meal had been despatched as a sordid necessity, they went forth into the forest—and what work of God is there to equal a Russian forest in summer? There they idled away the afternoon, hiding themselves far up, almost near the source of the little brook, where the other people came not, neither the screech-voiced matrons lamenting the scarcity of things in proportion to the numerousness of their offspring—neither they nor the mischievous boys with their lungs of iron, and all was quiet as in heaven. Only once Bylah felt her heart stop because she thought that through the foliage she descried the sullen, peering face of Gedaliah. But what was there to dread? Was he not with her, her lord of the strong right arm? and did she not feel his head cradled on her lap even while she glanced for a moment at the twinkling brooklet that was making such gigantic efforts to leap over the mound of pebbles barring its course at the bend? And all the time her hands were revelling among the tangle of his hair; could there be a greater delight

REDEMPTION OF THE SERPENT

than that? Besides, it kept her fingers employed, for they were itching to cull the crocuses and "lion-mouths" that encompassed them, and that would be breaking the Sabbath, for it came within the degree of manual labour. It was all so different to the bygone days, when Bylah had to sit through an afternoon like this, not romping with the other girls on the meadows, but reading out to grandmother the apocryphal wonders set forth in the musty pages of the "Go-and-See-Book"; and when she had drudged near to the end, grandmother would wake up and ask to have the reading repeated from the point where she dozed off; and as she was not sure of the place, to prevent mistakes Bylah had to begin at the beginning. Poor old grandmother! it was now three months since she had ceased pretending to be awake and had gone to sleep in earnest. And at the memory of it all, Bylah lifted up her voice and sang the song from "Shulamith," the one that is called the "Almond-and-Raisin Song"; and Aryah, looking up with swimming eyes, repeated the refrain under his breath :

> "So think of it, waking or sleeping,
>   The vow, that is ours for our own:
> Through days of rejoicing and weeping,
>   I love thee, thou lov'st me, alone."

And the song ran on, and the brook ran on, and the time ran on till it was dark, and they rose to return through the forest amid the sacred sounds and silences of the night.

That was in the summer; but presently the season grew tired of its glare and glory, and became ill-tempered and whimsical. A haggard look lay upon the trees, and the sun felt chilly and retired early to bed. Towards the end of the autumn Bylah and Aryah moved two villages further up country, for that was more central to the circuit wherein lay his best custom. But even then the way was still very long, and the north wind is an awkward fellow when you have him for your out-rider, much more when you meet him face to face, and Aryah came home not always pleased with the day's work nor with the prospects of the morrow. Not that he abated in his kindness to Bylah, but his manner was a little fretful, and now and then, what had never happened before, he made wry mouths at the dishes she set before him. And then came the long evenings, which Aryah got through somehow by dint of much yawning and stretching, and rolling of cigarettes, while Bylah sat knitting warm winter stockings for his use and talked. But there was a furtive watchfulness about her eyes as she looked at him that gave a discordant undertone to her light-hearted prattle. They knew no one in the place, for Aryah had no time to make friends, and Bylah no inclination. What were friends to her when she had Aryah?

And all through Aryah made no complaint; but when one night in the early part of the winter there was a knock at the door and Gedaliah stamped in, shaking the snowflakes off his coat and hat, Aryah jumped up with a little cry of joy.

"Blessed be your coming," he said, reaching out an eager hand; "why, I should not be more surprised to see Elijah the prophet actually step into my room on Passover night when the best and greatest in Israel are asking him to be their guest."

"Thanks for the greeting," replied

Gedaliah; "it feels good to be made welcome in the dwellings of others; what is the saying? 'Bind me by all fours and cast me among my friends.' How goes it with you, Bylah?"

But Aryah cut short her answer, and took entire possession of Gedaliah, asking him about their acquaintances, the object of his coming, and many other things. And so he learned that Gedaliah had various matters of import—he did not specify them—to transact in the neighbourhood, and that he would stay some time in the village; and Aryah clapped his hands at the news. Bylah had settled down again to her work, but her fingers moved more quickly in proportion to the quickening of her heart's pulse. And thinking rapidly, many thoughts came in her mind—her distrust of the man and the strangeness of his arrival; the memory of the Sabbath afternoon when he had followed them, as she thought, to spy upon their happiness; and at that a tear gathered in her eye, for she could not but feel that things were not all they had been in those golden days. It did not escape her, that tremor of gladness in her husband's voice at the appearance of their guest and at the tidings that he would not depart immediately. She was then no longer all in all to him, that his heart must needs turn to others to be filled with pleasure. She could not understand it. And then again she reproached herself for her fancifulness. What after all had she against the man? Had he not taken his rebuff in good part, and troubled her no more when he knew her mind? As for her husband, he might well be wearied for a little time with the surfeit of her presence. She had nothing to offer him besides her infinite love and patience, and he was a man, and his thoughts ranged beyond the boundary of her world. Assuredly it was better thus; his heart would come back to her with double eagerness when it had become chilled in the keeping and contact of others.

Meanwhile the two men talked, raking up old memories they had in common, and so far had they progressed in their intimacy, that when Gedaliah left and his host saw him to the door, it was "boon-comrade" and "brother-heart" between them at every second word, and Gedaliah was straitly enjoined to come again the following evening. Next morning Aryah's face was a little brighter, and before starting he kissed his wife three times, to make up for one or two occasions whereon lately he had neglected the act. Bylah took it as it came, nor did she harp too much on the thought that he was kind to her for the sake of another. Rarely is there much to be gained by reading between the lines, and in a woman's case it means wrinkles which do not act as love-charms. And, true to his word, Gedaliah came at night, and not alone. In his hand he bore a flask of corn-brandy, and as he set it on the table he said, with a laugh:

"Fear not, Aryah, it is of a good sort, and clean; nor is the seal upon it Rabbi Yochanan's ban of excommunication."

And he knew why he said that, for Aryah would be sure to ask him the story, which was famous throughout the province, though none knew the right and wrong of it; and Gedaliah was great in telling stories of wit and wickedness, especially those wherein he had had a hand. And this particular story was how Rabbi Yochanan of Stolp had prohibited Gedaliah from selling wines and spirits because they were profaned for use, having passed through the hands of Gentiles in the manufacture. Now this was a great loss to Gedaliah, who dealt chiefly among those who adhered strictly to the faith. So, being eager for revenge, and having ascertained one day that Rabbi Yochanan was going to a wedding feast in an outlying hamlet, he went to the first place through which the Rabbi would have to pass, and told the people—mujiks all of them—that he came as the forerunner of a great juggler and acrobat; but one who needed great stress put upon him ere he would display aught of his craft and cunning. And thus when Rabbi Yochanan arrived at the place he found many people assembled, who stopped his horses and bade him alight. And he did so, wondering what it all meant. Then they told him to make exhibition of his skill; but the poor little pot-bellied ecclesiastic stood gaping at them bewildered, till a whip cracked and a lash across his shoulders told him they were in earnest. And finding no escape, he steadied himself with one hand against the wall, and stood first on one leg and then on the other; but when he made an attempt at hopping, he toppled over and lay all his length on the floor. Then the peasants grew angry, and told him unless he did something worth looking at evil would befall him. So in his distress he called his driver, who knew more of the affair than he would tell his master, and said: "See here, Moyshaaron, I will place my head on the ground, and do thou push from the rear, so that I may turn head-over-heels and make sport for these murderers." Moyshaaron did his best, but even then the attempt was a failure, and with hooting and cudgelling the peasants seized hold of the Rabbi and pitched him back into his waggon, together with a cargo of mud and much refuse vegetables. And the whole thing Gedaliah wound up with the declaration: "And this, forsooth, is to show thee, brother mine, that it is my custom not to rest till I have brought hurt upon those who have acted contrariwise to my desire." Aryah heeded not the moral, for he was too busy wriggling with laughter; but Bylah heard it, and it

REDEMPTION OF THE SERPENT 77

seemed to her that the words were not spoken at random.

Now the telling of the tale had taken a long time, and by the end of it the brandy flask felt somewhat relieved of its contents; nor was Aryah remiss in helping its depletion. All through the evening it was but rarely that he cast his eyes in the direction where Bylah sat, or he would have seen that the louder he laughed the lower drooped her head, so that the glistening stains on her cheek might not be seen. And at last Gedaliah went away with his empty bottle and the promise, which was not empty, to come earlier next day, for Aryah said he would only go three-quarters of his ordinary round.

So it came about that Gedaliah and his brandy bottle became a nightly institution in Aryah's household; and Aryah was ever shortening his hours of labour so that he might be home the sooner. Bylah saw how Gedaliah was growing more and more a necessity with him; but she wept her tears in silence, and made him no reproaches. And about four weeks after the intruder's first appearance she was taken ill. She had gone one morning to the pump—for the water-carrying and wood-chopping had been left to her for some time—and, hatchet in hand, she began cutting away the ice that crusted thickly round the place. For the frost-fiend had been busy all night decorating the village-monument in question with designs that particularly struck his fancy, and when he saw her making havoc of his handiwork he grew angry, and in passing laid his finger on her bosom—lightly, it is true, but sufficient to chill the marrow in her bones, so that she kept her bed with the ague. Aryah was very good to her, and brought her warm potions and appliances, and sat with her—till Gedaliah came, and no longer. Her apartment was separated from the main room by a thin partition, and so she could hear most of what was going on there. And on the fourth day of her sickness, when it was at its height, soon after Gedaliah's entrance, she heard a sound coming from the other chamber that made her leap up in terror. The men were talking low, but between the words she caught the "swish-swish" of cards being shuffled—for Aryah had not been bold enough to defile her eyes with the sight of what he knew she hated most on earth; but now that she was out of the way, what harm was done? And again she listened eagerly to ascertain what the game was; it was not "frantsa-foos," nor "clabberyas"—to be sure it was "okka," the deadly, ruinous "okka." Now of all the thousand combinations in which the paste-boards may be manipulated, "okka" is pre-eminently the fabrication and pet child of the devil. It blends cunning and accident in a way more curious than any other game, and it is the spade that has dug the grave for the prosperity of many a household. You only use the pack from the nines upward, deal to each player two cards turned down and two cards face up; and then you must scrape together every item of mother wit, and every atom of Providence that has been set aside to watch over your undeserving head, if you would escape from the clutches of an expert player with unscathed skin; and Gedaliah was an expert player. Therefore it astonished Bylah very much to hear Aryah say at the finish of the play: "Gedaliah, you must look to your reputation, for I have won from you the best part of two roubles." But when Aryah came to her room on tiptoe she feigned to be asleep, for she would not shame him with her knowledge of his doings. This went on till she had strength enough to move about again, and then happened what her woman's heart had prophesied her; for Aryah, to escape the embarrassment of her presence, changed the scene of the gambling to Gedaliah's house, just coming home to deposit his wares and to swallow a hasty meal. But however late he returned for the night, Bylah made no comment, for she was too proud for bickerings and remonstrances, nor would she beg for the love that was not given her willingly. Often she wondered what kept Gedaliah in the neighbourhood, for he had no apparent business, and was ever loitering aimlessly about the village; but she was to know soon.

One morning, when Aryah was out hawking, she saw Gedaliah make a nonchalant entrance; he had not been in her house for some time now, and even when they saw each other not a word had passed between them.

"You seem lonely, Bylah," he began.

REDEMPTION OF THE SERPENT

"I have come to bear you company, though you do not look thankful for the good office." He spoke lightly, but he stepped back quickly enough as he saw her turn her blazing eyes upon him.

"You have done your best to make me lonely and an outcast from mine own," she answered, controlling herself; "am I to thank you for that?"

"I have made you lonely?" he repeated, in apparent wonderment; "but it must be true, since it is your own mouth that says so. Strange it is that the man for whose sake you denied my suit thinks so little of his good fortune."

"Gedaliah," said Bylah, quietly, "it is foolish of you to mock me, for I cannot feel aught you say. My heart is dead and I am dead, and it is lost labour to stab at something that does not writhe at the stroke. But go hence, before I curse you —the curses of the dead come true."

"I am cursed enough," said Gedaliah, lightly; "I game and I drink, and truly there must be an evil doom upon me, for those that consort with me cannot but do the same."

"An evil doom and a perdition you

have been to him," was Bylah's answer to the taunt; "you have made him what he is—and on the Day of Judgment I shall demand him of you as he was; and beware if you cannot answer the demand."

But at her words a change came over Gedaliah's face, and he took a step towards her. "Why talk of him at all, Bylah?" he said, caressingly. "He loves you no longer; he treats you like a dog. All his love has gone forth to me; but I have husbanded it carefully, and here I offer it to you. Take it, and me therewith; I can give you two men's love, and now you have neither's. Come with me, Bylah, and I shall worship you; you can get the divorce easily, I shall take that upon me; come—only come."

She looked at him for a moment, and then burst into a laugh that went rasping across his soul and lacerated it in a thousand places. And still shrieking with laughter, she ran into the adjoining room and shot the bolt. That was all the answer he got from her; but from the threshold he turned back once more and flung these words at her:

"Did you mark what I said that day of

my habits of revenge? Is it an idle boast? You can tell, surely, if any one, for you have not only learned the lesson, but lived it. And if I have made him different from of old, I shall make him so that his own good angel shall not recognise him on the day he stands in the gates of death."

When Aryah came home at night, Bylah told him simply:

"Gedaliah was here, and cast insult upon me; he would have me come and be a wife unto him."

But Aryah flared up:

"What nonsense thou talkest; what is thy head made of that thou canst not see a jest? Would he say such a thing in earnest? A man may turn his eye upon a woman without having it in his heart to deal evil with her—so much for thy wisdom. And now haste thee about the meal, for I am hungry." And then he ate his food in silence and went to Gedaliah as usual.

As Bylah said, her heart was indeed dead within her; but the numbed sullenness of her despair lived through all those dreary and desolate days and nights. And now and then the twin-demon of fury and helplessness lashed her forth to lurk like a wounded beast in the outskirts of Gedaliah's dwelling. At last, almost by instinct, she had found an opening in the hedge whence she could peer in through the window. At first glance she thought she had mistaken the house, for certainly there sat Gedaliah, but the other man's face she knew not. The thing that crouched there with glazen eyes and drooping jowl was not her Aryah. And so she watched them almost interestedly—for the two men seemed to her as strangers with whom she had no concern. She noted how that all the time Gedaliah held and dealt the cards, which showed, according to the rules of the game, that he was winning, and further she noted how he shuffled them with the tantalising deliberateness of a man who holds the key of a situation and knows it. And each time he saw the frantic eagerness wherewith his opponent clutched at his cards, there flitted across Gedaliah's face a smile all contempt and exultation that was more terrible than the other man's despair.

So deal succeeded deal to the unvarying advantage of Gedaliah; if Aryah had thirty-one, Gedaliah had three nines, or three queens or three kings. But at last there came a hitch in the game, and Bylah held her breath, for the play was running very close, and both players were confident of victory; and the staking and counter-staking went higher and higher.

"Three aces," said Aryah, with a deep breath, and laid his hand on the pool. "Not so fast," remarked Gedaliah, calmly, and showed up: he had four of a colour. Aryah sprang up with an oath, and putting his hand in his pocket he took out a small casket and threw a gold coin on the table. "The last!" he shouted. Bylah started back with affright and eagerly felt in the folds of her dress. The key was gone, the key of the little stronghold that held her savings. Not the money—not the money she cared for; but Aryah had become a thief. And next morning the people of the village asked each other with scared faces if they had heard the wail of unhuman sorrow that had passed their houses last night, and every man looked to his doorpost amulet to see if it was sound and would keep out the evil spirits.

It was on the third night after her vision of hell, as it had seemed to Bylah. For once she sat up; she did things mechanically now, and that interfered with her previous habits. She kept no count of time; why should she? What was there to expect or to hope for? Her life had again become the immeasurable nothingness it had been before; so let it be, since that was to be her fate. And suddenly she heard steps outside, and a man breathing heavily came along the passage and pushed open the door. It was Gedaliah, and on his shoulder he carried something; and Bylah thought calmly, from the mode of his carrying, that his practice as contraband-porter came him in good stead.

"Quick," he gasped; "help me put him to bed; he must be kept warm—the cold may have already done him harm."

Without a word she rose to his bidding and helped him to cover up the heaving mass and wiped the foam from the quivering lips. She supposed it was Aryah, or else why should this thing have been brought to her house? And Gedaliah caught her questioning look and told her: "It came upon him suddenly; it was the brandy, I think; but he would not stop, and flung me away as I strove to wrest the bottle from his hand. There is no danger if he be well tended, and when he is recovering no doubt he will send me news thereof, and I shall come again. Say, am I not keeping my word?" And then he turned to go; but as he clasped the door handle there was a loud sobbing from the middle of the room, and there was Bylah crawling to him on her knees with outstretched arms, and all the pent-up anguish of many days flowed unrestrainedly from her lips:

"Gedaliah, by the life of your mother and your sisters and all the womankind that is of your flesh and blood, let not the hand of your vengeance choke all the happiness out of my life. I have disdained you, I have preferred to you another; but in your mercy remember I am of human make, and it was God's will, not mine, that swayed me in my desires. Though you have sinned every day of your life, though you have violated all the ordinances of earth and heaven, let not go this chance of winning your redemption. Spare me and spare my husband, and take away from him the curse of your temptation, as you hope to clasp a loving wife to your bosom and to lead your children beneath the bridal canopy. I beseech you, Gedaliah, upon your hope of the World-to-come, I beseech you, look, here in the dust." And with that she grasped the edge of his tunic and buried her face therein.

Long did Gedaliah stand looking down on her, and devil and angel wrestled in his heart for the mastery. But at last he laid his hand gently on her head and said: "Bylah, you have conquered, and I am prostrate in the very hour of my triumph; I give him back to you, and when I am gone hence he will love you as of yore. But I loved you too—look how I loved you." And he took out a piece of parchment and held it before her; but she waved it away, signing to him to read its purport. And this is what it contained:—

"I, Aryah Klenker, herewith bind myself to be a bondslave unto Gedaliah Ickroner, and my wife Bylah likewise to be a handmaiden unto the same; and he shall deal with us as is his pleasure for a period of two years."

"See, Bylah," Gedaliah continued, "this

is how I love you," and the paper fluttered in fragments at her feet. "And now good-bye," and he stooped and kissed her once on the forehead; "and when Aryah awakes, give him my brotherly love—and this." It was a heavy purse of money. "It is his own, he but lent it to me for a while." And then he went out pensively and slowly, like a man who is afraid of treading on the tail of his thoughts.

And Bylah had a weary time of it for a week. Aryah raved and raved, and his utterances were all confused. "Gedaliah— that is the wrong card, I saw thee shifting it;—but you may believe me, good sir, that I speak truth: this leather is not catskin, but good Ukraine bullock; nay, take not thy hand away, Bylah, the sun comes stabbing through the trees—not drink, Gedaliah? may I not drink for the last time that I am a free man and not a servant? and now, one kiss more, Bylah, before——" And so it went on till one day he opened his eyes without a film on them, and fancied himself in Paradise, for over there stood Bylah, and she, or the heavenly hosts, were singing the refrain from the "Almond-and-Raisin Song:

> "Through days of rejoicing and weeping
> I love thee, thou lov'st me, alone."

"I have had a bad dream, Bylah," he said feebly, "but I am better now ; it was all about Gedaliah, the smuggler we knew in our native village, and we were doing all manner of strange things ; come close, sweetheart—nay, closer. But what is this ? One must not mix wine and water, for it is foolish of thee to laugh and cry at the same time."

THE MIGRATION OF SAINT SEBASTIAN

"IT'S an ill wind that blows nobody good," runs the time-honoured saying, and will probably continue to run till the end of all things. Proverbs are the pack-asses that carry the worsted and the homespun philosophy of the world across the continents of the commonplace. Poor patient proverbs—poor patient pack-asses; and the strangest thing of all is that they occasionally convey a truth. Of their miscarriages and aberrations no notice is taken. So much the worse for them; for each time they come home to their event it is counted new evidence that they are fit for their purpose, and that saddles them with a new lease of service. With regard to the especial burden and bearing of the above-mentioned pack-ass—I mean proverb—if you wish to discover it, you will have to follow it all the way to the confines of Tartary and the Greek Catholic Calendar; and as the way is long, you had better draw a good breath before starting.

The journey's end will bring you to one of the villages hidden deep in the steppes of the Ukraine; for that is where they lived—these boys, rascals, or devils—you can specify them according to the intensity of your own love of goodness. Assuming them to be devils, their own proper and peculiar pandemonium was a military government institution which combined the characteristics of an orphanage with that of a penitentiary. By being open chiefly to orphan boys of officers it justified its claim to the one title; Draconian severity of regulations made it the other. Not that such was not necessary. Had the reins of control been one degree slacker, the very saints and angels would have wished Paradise a few thousand fathoms higher; but old Colonel Schubyakowski, the governor, took good care that the existing proportions of the universe were not interfered with.

The more immediate purpose of the

institution was to furnish the crack regiments with recruits. The cadets, carefully picked as to fitness, were taken in hand from the age of seventeen, and taught the soldiering craft as their fathers had been taught before. Thus was the bone and blood of the old school to be perpetuated, and a race of dare-devils to be bred fit to lift the universe from its hinges; and the present crop was as promising as any of those that had preceded it, for it gave every indication of being the true seed of those centaurs of the plains, the Uhlans and Cossacks, who in the good old days, it was currently reported, were accustomed to sew up live cats in the bellies of their prisoners, and used babies for tent-pegging sport.

Just at present the inmates were in very bad humour, because things were so hopelessly dull. The whole life and soul seemed to have gone out of the place in the person of Ignatz Pablowitch—Ignatz their old and trusty leader, now conscribed to the service. The first few days they passed monotonously in respectable diversions, to wit, in pilfering the pyxes of the neighbouring churches, in stoning fishes writhing on the bank, in crucifying frogs and setting the bloodhounds on the track of Hebrew pedlars, or else helping the local knacker in his delectable work. But all these things were mere makeshifts, for they were used to occupations less elementary. True, there was a certain amount of domestic excitement, for with such inflammable substance things could not be expected to progress on the "love-in-a-dovecot" system; all the energy accumulated from want of external friction had to find an outlet, if only an internal one, and so they fell to mutual hair-pulling —not sportively, but after the manner of young giants extracting oaks by the roots. If a cranium got broken here or a shoulder put out of joint somewhere else, it was merely a lesson in the science of self-preservation; for having learnt the painfulness of the experience, one would do his best to forestall its re-occurrence, and there were few who did not get their fair share of learning. The governor shut an indulgent eye, for did not all this tend to make each one of them a human slaughter-machine in time of war?

The denizens of the institution were

cleft into two parties. The smouldering fire of discontent was fanned by the breath of faction, and now the question of leadership had stirred it into an open blaze. Without a leader they were nothing; nay, more, they were a mockery and derision to their inveterate foes—the ploughmen and field-labourers of the adjacent hamlets. Why, only the other day one of their comrades had been waylaid by the sheep-boys of Sompolka, who sent him home, his arms tightly pinioned and a mangy cur dangling fantastically from his neck; and all these indignities they suffered because of the interminable wrangling between Black Wolf and Dimitri. Neither of them would give way; both had equal claims to the captaincy, or, at least, equal determination to uphold them.

There had been hatred between these two ever since they could remember, with this difference, that Black Wolf did the hating and Dimitri allowed himself to be hated. Black Wolf's ill-feeling afforded Dimitri great satisfaction; he considered it a compliment, and returned it merely as a matter of courtesy. For Dimitri had good manners; indeed, there was something altogether superior about him in his well-formed features, white skin, and ivory teeth; whereas Black Wolf, with his bush of coal-black, gipsy hair, his bloodshot pig-eyes and saffron fangs, did not at first sight look prepossessing, and it scarcely needed a further acquaintance to develop this impression into utter repulsion. Perhaps it was for this that he hated Dimitri; he had only to appear in the distance, and the serving-maids, who stood gossiping round the village-pump, frantically clutched their half-filled pails with the cry, "Here comes Black Wolf," and stampeded, cackling and shrieking like a flock of geese that scent the fox. Nor was it likely he should improve his temper by prowling round the house of Father Ivanovitch and by peering through the cracks of the shutters, only to see Dimitri and little Marinka sitting with hands clasped before the cosy hearth. Of course he could have the pleasure of rattling at the window, just to make her shiver with dread of the night-witches, or of Vyeej, the iron-wrought fiend, who is not deterred even by the sign of the cross, because his eyelids reach right down to the ground, so that he can see nothing ; but it only made the girl cling closer to her lover, and Black Wolf scurried away into the darkness with curses on his lips. Often had he gone down on his knees and prayed to his patron : " Dear, good Saint Sebastian, slay Dimitri quickly, and I shall ever after observe thy name-day with fasting and prayer." Some people want their deity to be merely their worse *alter ego.* At any rate St. Sebastian knew that he could not jeopardise his position in the Calendar by turning assassin, and at last Black Wolf grew sulky with him and resolved to have his revenge on the saint no less than on Dimitri.

As regards the latter, a good deal of the prestige that clung to him originated in the mystery surrounding his derivation. Nobody, not even he himself, knew who he was or whence he had emanated ; he had been smuggled into the Government House without possessing the proper qualifications, and in the transit he had apparently lost his patronymic, for he was never called anything else but just " Dimitri." In default of a more tangible clue, conjectures as to his history attached themselves to the livid circle that ran round his neck. By some it was considered a mark for ultimate identification; others whispered that it testified to the efforts of a high-born dame to dispose of an unwelcome encumbrance—that the noose, however, had been tied by unskilful fingers, and a woodchopper who was passing through the forest had cut the infant down in time to save its little life. Others again maintained, pessimistically, that the mark was evidence that Dimitri was doomed to be hanged. Dimitri treated this gossip with cordial indifference; he laughed, and said it was not likely that one who had commenced life by nearly being strangled, should end it in the same manner—that would be too much of a coincidence. And so the matter of his origin was left pending.

It was now the tenth day since the departure of Ignatz, and the universe was yet at a standstill. For want of something better there had been a wholesale departure to the nearest valley-hollow to yawn away the tediousness of a dog-day afternoon. Life was a blank with no immediate future and an interminable present. Each side cursed the pig-headedness of the other in not coming to an understanding, and studiously resolved not to be the first to make advances. Black Wolf lay sullenly on his stomach, every now and then angrily tossing his head as it came into contact with the prickly grass blades; it was near haytime, and the foils, curled and sapped by the sun's fierceness, stung like spears. Furtively he watched Dimitri where he lay, seemingly at peace with the whole world, ensconced in a recess of the valley that overhung him with projecting ledge, and cradled him like a solicitous mother on a couch of spring-green moss. Dimitri seemed to have the best in everything, and this complacency wherewith he accepted his good fortune frenzied Black Wolf to desperation. Now or never—he must put an end to this, come what may.

"Oh, ye blocks of idleness," he shouted, jumping up, "are we to lie thus till old age and doomsday overtake us? Look, our flesh is getting soft to melting, like that of girls, and our bones are crumbling away with the rot of sloth. I cannot forget that I was born a man, if you have forgotten."

The disconsolate day-dreamers started up at the sound of his voice; it was as though a thunderbolt had crashed into the turf on which they lay, and had cleft it into a blackened rent before their eyes; and in wonder they pricked up their ears to listen to the storm of which this must be the precursor. There were few amongst them, besides Black Wolf, who could presume to break in so rudely upon their siesta. But no better time could be chosen to betray them into sudden action; rack the apathy of an undecided man to its utmost power of tension, and you will get him to roll among nettles for sheer distraction.

"And all because one man has left you?" Black Wolf continued, passionately; clearly he was infuriating himself by his own words. "I speak not of your pride —that is dead—but what of your prudence? Here we go shifting at random, like fluff in the wind, and our strength grows faint for want of a hand to nourish it. And still you do not seek it; wait on— and perhaps Michael, the archangel, will come down to you after he has put the heavenly hosts through their exercises."

And while Black Wolf was still laughing bitterly at his impious jest, into which he perverted the teachings of good Father Ivanovitch, a stir ran through the gathering. The isolated little heaps of indolence lifted and shifted themselves, gravitated towards one another according to their motive, coagulated into little knots, which again confounded themselves into larger clusters, until the straggling groups had become compacted into two solid arrays that faced each other, with a Rubicon between them. So the crisis had come at last, and each man had chosen his cause and his leader. Black Wolf glanced from his followers over to Dimitri's, as a thresher looks from the grain to the chaff; but he was vexed that the quantities should be so equal.

"Now I can speak," he continued his harangue; "some one—I will not say who—has divided us in strife against ourselves. There has been underhand speech, and much backbiting to set us by the ears, and to seize the leadership during the tumult; but all this shall avail nought, for I, and none other, shall be your leader, by right of valour and descent. Who can count more generations of his line that grew into soldiers over there than I?" and he pointed to their *alma mater;* "or, if any one thinks he has a better claim, let him stand forth, and I will argue with him."

There was truth in what Black Wolf had said. His great-grandfather had been one of the aboriginal inmates, and that made Black Wolf, so to speak, a foundationer of the place; and Dimitri was a mere foundling, an intruder without name or history.

Black Wolf looked round insolently, waiting for an answer, and when none came, he continued, with a smile of disdain:

"Do you see how it is? When the mischief is done, one stoops one's head and lets the challenge hurtle over it."

No one mistook the point of the remark, least of all Dimitri, and Dimitri was playing his game as he thought best, and so he answered:

"And if one may ask," he said, lazily raising himself on his elbow and motioning those in front to stand away—for through all the agitation he had not stirred from his place—"if one may ask, what would be the manner of your arguing?"

"Oh, by casting of sheep's eyes and fondling of hands by the chimney," sneered Black Wolf; "that would suit you, would it not? I prefer letting bone speak to bone and sinew to sinew."

Of course Dimitri had known all along what Black Wolf meant; he knew also that Black Wolf was a formidable advocate in arguments of that sort—his chest looked alarmingly broad and his arms were uncompromisingly long. Moreover, when he was in earnest he could bite out pieces of flesh with the best of his four-footed namesakes; and Dimitri thought if that happened in his case there would be less of him to kiss, and Marinka would not like it. Perhaps his motive was less disinterested, but no one could have told whether the flicker at the corner of his mouth was a tremor of fear or a stray sunbeam gliding across it, and his voice sounded hard and straight as a ramrod.

"Black Wolf," he said, slowly, "yours is a fool's carcase, and your head is stuffed with bran and oats. First, it was by no insidious talk that I gained the favour of those that wish me well; and therein you have spoken lyingly. Nor, again, is it by the strength of our single arms that this matter can be decided. Suppose you turn out to be the stronger, or I—what does that show? Nothing, except that one of us is fitter for carrying burdens than the other; and at that a three months old ox would excel us. Strength without wisdom is like an axe without a handle; and in a leader a ready wit is more than a ready blow."

This was a home-thrust for Dimitri, for every one knew that his presence of mind had helped them out of many a scrape into which the hot-headed Wolf had hurried them. The latter stood writhing with annoyance; he thought the trap was fast, and here he saw his enemy wriggling out of it and mocking him for his clumsiness.

"God send me to deal with men, and not with children that prate like women," he cried, impatiently; and then he continued, maliciously: "Say, Dimitri, did your father teach you all this wisdom while dandling you on his knee?"

Dimitri showed a calm face, despite his inward quailing at the taunt; he got up, and nonchalantly stepping into the middle he said:

"Comrades mine, 'where there is folly there is selfishness,' is the saying, and Black Wolf has proved it just now. He has taken this matter into his own hands, and has lost count of you altogether, as though you were mere puppets to dance at his bidding. But I say, this is for you to consider, and if I speak at all, it is not to burst your ears with loud words, but to help you to your decision. Now this is my plan: we are evenly matched as to numbers, so that none can say this is a case of an iron hammer against a glass anvil; let us, then, fight the matter out in open battle, and let the rest go by the issue—that would be fairer, as I take it."

And the long and short of it was that they decided to have a grand scrimmage on the following day, and the leader of the victorious side was to be accorded the dignity of generalissimo. Dimitri's proposal was popular; it meant a chance of settling private feuds, of clearing the atmosphere generally, and, finally, it was one, and by no means the worst, way of unscrewing the deadlock.

Black Wolf hung back moody and thoughtful in the wake of the crowd that surged homeward clamorously. He did not at all like the way things had turned out; he knew he was no general, and that was why he had been so anxious to settle the affair by single combat, for Dimitri was a wily trickster and excelled in matters of strategy. And so Black Wolf felt very diffident as to the result; but perhaps the arm of Providence could be given a little push in the right direction. He needed not dirty his own fingers for it —these things belonged to the province of Nicolai and his likes. Nicolai would do it; Nicolai did everything that every one else fought shy of: he ate apples from the dust-heap, he spat on crucifixes, and committed all the iniquities that lay between these two extremes. They called him Toadmouth, and a man must be possessed of one or two disagreeable habits at least before he can deserve the sobriquet; and that is why he was now straggling on the outskirts of the throng and no one cast a look towards him. He had taken Wolf's side, not from any preference, but because if he did not take one side, he would be battledored between the two. And now when he felt a hand on his shoulder, and, in turning, found himself looking into Wolf's face, he gave a little scream, and ducked as though he were hamstrung.

"This way, Toadmouth," Wolf said, dragging him behind a hedge; "keep still, till the others have gone, and when your teeth have stopped chattering perhaps you will be able to hear what I tell you."

It did not take Black Wolf long to make his meaning clear to Toadmouth; the latter was quick-witted as a fox where mischief was concerned, and any opposition to Wolf's proposal meant mischief to himself. So they discussed the matter for a long time, and then Wolf said to the other, as a final injunction:

"You will find one at the shambles; get the strongest you can pick, but not too large to go into the sleeve of your coat; you must not even let the tip be seen. Do you remember how he made you turn somersaults to show us Marinka's white teeth as she was laughing?"

Toadmouth remembered the incident quite well, and to drive it from his mind he took a stroll into the town, casually dropped in at the slaughter-house, and still more casually stole from there a cow-horn. Then he grew yet more mysterious in his doings, for he laid himself in a mud-puddle, and wallowed therein like a hog with the St. Vitus's dance; furthermore, he ripped open his breeches as far as the knee-joint, then he spent ten minutes in rehearsing an elaborate limp, and thus came whimpering like a mongrel to Dimitri:

"Black Wolf has beaten me within an inch of my life, because I would not steal him a sausage from the Poppe's larder; and I would not do it because you love Marinka, his daughter. Shield me, Dimitri, and I will serve you to-morrow among your most faithful."

And Dimitri, at the bidding of his destiny, made him welcome.

It was not often that the inmates had to resort to such extreme measures to settle a point; but provision had been made for the emergency, and a code of athletic warfare had been laid down which included only the exercise of weapons which nature had furnished. But a peculiar and favourite item was the nape-stroke; it consists of a knuckle-rub down the vertebræ which rasps on the nerves and seems to tear their network to tatters; and because it concentrates all the weakness of a man's body into his weakest part, it will, if dexterously administered, cripple him instantly. Two men are necessary for it as a rule, one to do the gripping from the front and the other the rasping at the back. Otherwise they mimicked the business of war very faithfully, even to the holding of court-martials and the takings of prisoners, who became serfs to their captors until by length of fag-service they had redeemed their freedom. Of course, these proceedings were entirely unofficial, and Governor Schubyakowski was not invited to honour them with his presence.

Dimitri did not sleep much that night, and his brain revolved busily. He had to make up his plan of campaign; these things could not be left to the last moment. Two courses were open to him — open battle and guerilla warfare. It depended on him what form the contest should take, for he knew Black Wolf would wait to see what he did and then do the same. So he decided on open battle, for that left him more master of initiative. Besides, Black Wolf was rash; something could be counted on that. A little ambush or so, just simple enough to escape suspicion, would go a long way, at least a longer way than Black Wolf could see before him. And at last, through the leaden heat-haze that half numbed his brain, Dimitri could see the thread of an idea; and with a little more weaving of thought the thread became a cord, and the cord a rope, that, if all went well, would fetter Black Wolf hand and foot. Dimitri was satisfied; he had simply not to oversleep himself in the morning; after that the complications would begin.

And rise early he did; and not long afterwards the dormitories were astir and buzzing with the excitement of events that seemed too big for speech. Unmerciful inroads were made on the morning meal, for the day was likely to be a heavy and hungry one. Then Dimitri passed the word; his followers were quick to the call and they sallied forth, jauntily treading the buoyant morning air, and stringing tight a muscle or two that might have become slack with disuse. And then one of them started the soldier-song which Kavischko, the great bard, had imported with him when they brought him prisoner from Tcherkessia, and the strains of the "Blood Harvest" song rose in weird, uncouth cries like those of men who are being turned into beasts. And this is how it begins:

> "Blood is the bounty of God,
>   Blood is the blessing of men,—
> Quickens the seed in the clod,
>   Ripens the wheat in the fen.
>
> Feed ye your soil with the slain,
>   Each little trickle of red
> Grows you a bushel of grain,
>   Brings you a garner of bread."

Dimitri walked on, but he did not join in. The singing did them no harm—if they sang a little more courage into themselves, all the better; that was their business, not his. He had to think for them, and singing comes easily only to the thoughtless. Something had been gained already; he had succeeded in forestalling

Black Wolf in the matter of position. Dimitri could make his choice, and thus the necessity of the attack would be left to the enemy. So on they went, till the plain began to rise, and as it rose the voices of the clamorous crowd behind him sank lower, for their breath came more quickly and shortly with the ascent. Another quarter of an hour, and they had reached the high level of the tableland which Dimitri had chosen for action. For hundreds and hundreds of yards it stretched, till the edge of it became bounded off by a skirting edge of hazel-rods, matted and knotted together, and not growing upright, but slanting over like the beard of a man's chin when he is on his back. On the other side they overlooked the famous sand-hills of Sovarno that lead the slope steeply down again to the plain, and where the sand-diggers come from far and wide to dig the soft, shining sand which they cart about for sale in the villages. Here and there the earth was burrowed into huge deep cauldrons, so that a stranger might have thought he was in a country of troglodytes. But with these slopes Dimitri was not at present concerned, though he involuntarily felt if his neck was where it ought to be after the head-over-heel tumble they had given him two years ago as he was searching for birds' nests in the copse. But it was then that he discovered that the drooping fringe of hazel-willows over-canopied a terrace or ledge, about two feet wide, three-quarters the height of a man, from the top-level of the plain. It would give a firm foothold, and by tightly grasping the bushes one could easily provide against a precipitous descent to the hill-base, fathoms and fathoms below. It would serve his purpose admirably.

Dimitri ordered a halt, and his men sank sprawling on the ground, eagerly quaffing the freshening breeze that had sought refuge on the grassy height from the burning sands at the bottom, for the sun, despite the early hour, was already in violent mood. There was nothing to be done but to wait, and that also came not amiss, for it gave them time to rest; the enemy's scouts would have no difficulty in discovering them. Dimitri spent the time in speaking secretly to a dozen or so of his men on whom he could rely more surely than the rest, and instructed them carefully in all the details of his plan.

After an hour's waiting the enemy hove in sight, and at a word from Dimitri the dozen crept on their bellies to the brink of the plateau and warily glided through the thicket till their feet touched the terrace; and the bushes hid them from view, even on the sand hillside, though no one could reach them from that quarter. The rods, as they clutched them, felt wiry and deep-rooted, and were well fitted for helping a leaping vault to the top when the time came. Toadmouth noted the manœuvre, but said nothing. By now Black Wolf had reached the beginning of the incline, and stopped, considering how to reach the high land at the back of Dimitri's column; but it was dangerous—they were too near the border, and might topple him over the height, which meant broken arms and legs. So nothing could be done but to deploy in front, leaving Dimitri the benefit of higher ground; and that was just what Dimitri had expected. In a moment his line was formed; but he himself stood with a little reserve body, stationed to guard prisoners, twenty yards away from the main column. Toadmouth had begged a place near him, because, he said, Black Wolf had threatened to throttle him if he met him in the thick of the fight.

After that things went rapidly. Black Wolf just massed his men into shape, put himself in the centre, and flung headlong forward like a battering-ram. What happened after that is a matter for conjecture; but what is likely to ensue when you have three hundred pairs of arms clutching and clawing at each other, and three hundred bodies straining and struggling? — and that is without counting the action of the feet: it certainly looked like business. At first there was a little attempt at shouting, but it soon settled down into the silence of men who are determined that deeds should tell their own tale. All the time Dimitri stood stock still, surveying the scene. His men did not begrudge his keeping himself out of harm's way; they knew they could trust him—the decisive moment had not come, and Dimitri was always at his greatest then. So they fought on doggedly. Black Wolf was chafing with rage to find Dimitri out of his reach. "The coward," he thought, "he hides his cowardice under the mask of strategy; why, if I were to keep treading on the body of the worm all day, I should not kill it—in the head lies its life." And he looked up and eagerly watched the little group at the top. And just then he saw Toadmouth stretching out his arm, as though he were exercising it, and he knew that the time had come.

And then he started wedging his way out into the open, and the men whom he had chosen his bodyguard followed closely in his track. Once free, he dashed past the enemy's flank, and tore furiously up the slope, making straight for Dimitri. Dimitri's heart beat a little faster—his plan was working grandly—Black Wolf was delivering himself into his hands, the improvident fool! And now Black Wolf was within a yard or two; already he felt his hot breath, already their arms had closed around each other for the wrestle: and Dimitri opened his mouth to give the sign to the ambush on the ledge—opened his mouth, and shut it again with a snap, while his voice turned a somersault in his throat. And that was not all, for in addition the sun exploded, ripping open the sky, and a thousand imps with smoke-blackened wings and faces fell out of it, snatched up the trunk of his body and whirled away with it in a thousand directions through space; only his head and legs lay disjointed on the ground.

"Mercy on me!" thought Dimitri, "the end of the world has come, and I have not had absolution." And ere the waves of oblivion had closed over him, he heard a voice—it sounded thousands of miles away, yet it seemed the voice of Toadmouth—crying: "Dimitri has fallen—fly all who can."

But Dimitri could not have lain senseless long, for as he revived Black Wolf had not finished pinioning his arms.

"What are you doing to me—where are my comrades?" he said, faintly, without moving and looking neither left nor right. "Did I ever have the strength to move and look about me?" he wondered in his heart.

"If you stand up you can see them scampering away downhill," said Black Wolf, maliciously. "I do not blame them for stretching their legs—it was unkind of you, Dimitri, to keep your friends cooped up so long on a two-inch foothold. But we have caught a few, and presently there will be fine sport to see them do the devil's skip."

Dimitri shuddered, for Black Wolf meant that they were to run the gauntlet of the Craven Field; and this again implied treading with naked feet among the lumber and litter of many years that lay there accumulated in piles of broken pewter and earthenware. But such was the law for prisoners taken in flight, for tail-turning was not to be encouraged.

Wolf reflected a little, then an ugly smile broke across his face.

"How far is it from here to St. Sebastian's Cross?" he asked, and some one answered that it was half an hour's easy marching.

"Then help him up," continued Wolf, pointing to Dimitri, "and come with me."

A groan wrung itself from Dimitri's lips: "Somebody has been driving iron nails into my back — long thin-pointed nails, and the bone behind seems all in splinters," he moaned, trying to twist his arm round under the coils. And so he reeled on, tottering to and fro like a drunken man; and when he lagged, they hustled him to increase his pace. And every minute had the weariness of a mile, and the road lengthened endlessly, till he thought he was going down, down, down with a sinking feeling of unfathomable depth. Black Wolf walked on deep in thought, and if his thoughts were as black as his looks, it boded ill for somebody.

And at last the wayside shrine of St. Sebastian was reached. The old saint looked down astonished at his unexpected visitors, for he only held receptions on fixed and stated occasions, when the pilgrims came from far and near to invoke his blessing and protection. Poor old fellow, he seemed more in need of it than his votaries, so woe-begone and chopfallen he looked; his very crucifix seemed to have lost all self-respect in its ragged coat of paint.

Wolf looked wickedly at the saint: "You will do it now, old fox, whether you would or would not," he said under his breath. And turning to Dimitri, who had sunk down at the foot of the cross, he jeered: "Up, up! how unmannerly to sprawl thus in front of a saint; get up, and make your reverence!"

Dimitri looked up and said wearily, "You mock me, Wolf—and yet it puzzles me; I know there is strength in your arms such as few men possess; but to break me in two with one hug as though I were a rotten twig——"

He stopped short and stared hard before him; for he had caught sight of Toadmouth, who found it difficult to keep out of evidence among the half-dozen whom Black Wolf had set aside for Dimitri's escort. And in Toadmouth's girdle stuck a cow-horn, that could not serve as a bugle, for the tip was raw and unbored; and the thing had clearly no business there. Dimitri tried painfully to think. Toadmouth here, next to Black Wolf, from whom he had hidden, because of his murderous threat: there was more in this than showed at first glance. Toadmouth had deserted from Black Wolf, and a traitor might easily prove treacherous; and then there was the cowhorn, and a cowhorn might easily break a man's back. And at last a light came over Dimitri.

"I see, I see," he shrieked, "this is how men are struck down from behind: for this did you come to fawn on me, you faithless dog! Oh, if I am but healed again, I will tear out your entrails with the same cursed cow-horn with which you have ground my bones to powder. And yet," he continued, turning a questioning look on Black Wolf, "this is your work too. I can see it by the scarlet on your face; it was you who hired this assassin, in his treachery lay your strength——"

But his power of speech failed him, and with a little gasp he fell back on his side. Black Wolf hid his confusion as well as he could under a garb of icy nonchalance.

"More wisdom, I suppose. Truly this is a fine invention," he said; "why not take defeat with a good grace, which is the next best thing to victory? I know nothing of cow-horns and treachery and such things, but I know that I have won the leadership on the very terms of your own suggestion; and further, that you are my prisoner. So make an end of it—down on your knees!"

"A faithful servant you will win by trapping him into captivity," sneered Dimitri; "if he has any manhood in him, he will rise in the night and strangle his master."

At this Wolf turned with a gesture of accusing to his companions. "Do you hear what this rebellious hound says? Strangle his master in his sleep? Why, it is of such stuff that they are made who raise their arms in enmity against our Little Father—long may he rule; we must not let the brood increase—there are too many of them as it is."

He snatched up a coil of rope, with nimble hands tied a noose, and slung one end over the arm of the crucifix. The others watched him in silence: what a shrewd fellow Black Wolf was after all. Was it not a clever manœuvre of him to force Dimitri into terrified submission? But Black Wolf had other thoughts; he was merely intent on his revenge, and however things turned out they might readily be ascribed to accident. So he went close up to his victim and said:

"Dimitri, three times will I summon you to give way and acknowledge me your chief; and at the third time your life is in your own hands."

Dimitri remained silent at the first two appeals, but at the third he raised himself

MIGRATION OF ST. SEBASTIAN

on his elbow, looked steadfastly at his tormentor and hissed :

"Sooner than I stoop before you, may the cholera eat into your vitals, and jackals make havoc of your parents' graves."

There was a howl like that of a wild beast—a rush—and Black Wolf had flung himself on Dimitri, had forced the noose about his neck, and with frantic straining was tugging him aloft ; and before any one could make him loosen his hold, Dimitri's feet were inches off the ground, his face was black, and the last few shivers were passing through his body. And that was the last of Dimitri, unless the limp inert mass that lay loosely on the heather counted for anything.

Little to do was made over the matter ; coroner's inquests are not in vogue in that part of the world. People talked for a little time about the strange end of Dimitri who had been driven to accomplish the fate which destiny had, so to speak, marked out on his body. Of course, the pessimists had a high old time of it, and nearly gouged people's eyes out with their "I told you so." A good many were scandalised : the sacrilegious wretch, he could find nothing worse on which to hang himself than the crucifix of good old St. Sebastian, who no doubt was greatly upset by the occurrence. But there they were mistaken. The sly old saint was chuckling with delight. The ill wind that blew the life out of Dimitri had blown good luck into his way. For now that his shrine had been profaned his worshippers had to locate him elsewhere, and the change of scene was a godsend, especially as the atmosphere in the vicinity of his old domicile was not what it used to be, since somebody had started a cemetery close by. The only persons who had a right to grumble were the pilgrims coming eastward from Pulk, for they had to walk two weary miles further, and the way to Urtava, whither the saint had been removed, was all uphill and led through clumps and undergrowths of prickly fir-bushes. Perhaps it should be stated, moreover, that the gleam of little Marinka's white teeth was not seen for many a day after.

THE ASCENT INTO HEAVEN

> God, oh make me strong of limb,
>   God, oh make me straight of mind ;
> Save me from untoward whim,
>   Keep me conscious of my kind.
> Teach me judge twixt sin and saint,
>   Not by faith of self-deceit,
> Lest Thy taintless skies I taint
>   As I climb with bleeding feet.
> Prayer of Reason.

THE parishioners all remarked upon it ; the cattle-dealers and hawkers that came from the hamlets around on market days, and took the opportunity of attending mass or receiving absolutions, went away shaking their heads ; and on their way home the matter was discussed in all its bearings.

"Aye, Father Stanislaus is very strange in his ways, even stranger than when I saw him last."

"His wife's death is beginning to tell on him."

"Stupid one; what wife ever sent her husband crazy by dying?"

"But remember he is a priest, and may only marry once by the canons of the Church."

"Then let him thank the canons of the Church instead of his own good fortune. When my first wife died, I wept for her; when my second died, I wept for the pig which I had to kill for the funeral meal; and when my third died, I wept because she had not left me a pig to kill. Women are a plague to a thrifty man."

"What, did you also notice his eyes?"

"Notice them? why he nearly stabbed me with them when he glanced at me for an instant."

"And I could have sworn that at one time he was watching the angels tuning their violins, and at another old Clovenhoof beating his grandmother; but when he did which I cannot tell."

"That is nothing to what happened to me. I asked him, 'How goes it in limb and body, your reverence?' And at that he groaned and beat his breast, and cried 'peccavi,' as though it were a sin to be reminded of the infirmities of the flesh."

"Perhaps—let me whisper in your ear—perhaps he is about to abjure the faith and turn Malakhan."

"Have a care over your tongue! The Malakhans do not believe in images, and I distinctly saw him kiss the feet of the Holy Mother seven times."

"Has it anything to do with his little boy Wladislav? Is the lad not turning out well? Poor little fellow, he looks wan and thin; I do not think there is much mischief in his heart."

"No, and he has no honey-licking of it since his mother died; but after all it is none of our business. Surely we have enough to sweep in our own stables."

On Sundays after service there would be more whisperings.

"Tell me, magister—you who know all the languages under the sun—in what tongue did the father preach this morning?"

"No language at all, neither Latin nor Hebrew, but good gibberish of his own; and then there was not much in what he said. He called himself names, saying that he was a cesspool of sin and iniquity, and that for thirty miles round there was not so much wickedness as lay in his one little finger."

"And he said nothing about me, and did not rate me soundly for my transgressions? Why do I pay him tithe if he does not take me to task in his sermons? How can I, an honest man, go through life with self-respect if I am not frequently called scoundrel and orphan-spoiler?"

"That may be as it is; but certainly he is most prodigal of self-reproach. I should not be thankful for so keen a sense of my failings, unless he lays claim to trespasses of which he is guiltless, so as to get credit for not having committed them."

"Ah, then he is a holy man and a prudent one as well."

But Father Stanislaus was not actuated by such mercenary motives. He had no intention of coquetting with heaven. And let the truth be known at once: there had lately come upon him a strange desire to qualify for a saint, not the imitation article made of clay, but a full-fledged saint whose attributes are pilgrimages and wax tapers. The father was not afraid of death—it was a thing that happened only once in every man's life; but after death came eternity, and that, from all accounts, was a long-winded affair and went on happening for ever. It might become monotonous in the end without a more definite occupation than beatified idleness. A saint usually had his hands full; there was always a drought or a murrain or a heart-broken lover to be looked after. Besides, what scope was there not in the matter of miracles! And on this point Father Stanislaus had some notions of his own; he would make all the other saints look mere amateurs—he would perform miracles to which those of the Exodus would be as skittles to pyramids; and thus would his memory be hallowed and revered by all men. Saint Stanislaus—how pretty it sounded.

So he set about his sanctification in the time-honoured way. He waited for the Annunciation: that came in the shape of Anushka's death. Not that people must, as a rule, wait for their wives to die before they can devote themselves wholly to godliness, but it was the first important event in his dull parochial life. It was also a parallel to many instances of canonisation in which the sanctified were God-forsaken heathens until domestic bereavement chastened them and helped them to quite a respectable place in the Calendar. And this was what had changed Father Stanislaus into the loose-girded, straggling-limbed cassockman of whom the parishioners spoke with misgivings; and this was the cause of his public self-humiliations, his antics of asceticism, and all the other irregularities of a man whose wits are overspun with cobwebs. In the meantime the dirt accumulated in the corners of his house, the crevices in the walls grew wider, and the straw hung in mildewy festoons across the ceiling.

For all that little Wladislav loved his father, and in the intervals of his idiosyncrasy his father loved him; but there was much bickering between the two when it came to meal-times. Father Stanislaus wished to ignore these, because they reminded him that he was still subject to human necessities; and then little Wladislav had to argue with him, and what made him most eloquent was the fact that his father kept the key of the pantry, and without the pantry there could be no dinner.

And possibly this abstinence had something to do with the fact that Father Stanislaus was haunted by apparitions. One night he sat up in his bed with a start, and awoke little Wladislav, who slept in a cot close by.

"Little son," he whispered, awestruck, "come here and chase away the ghost that stands looking at me from the foot of the bed."

"Which ghost, father?" said the little fellow, rubbing his eyes.

"There it stands, all white in its grave-clothes—quick, cast it out of doors!"

"But, father, that is the clothes-rack with your surplice on it."

"It was a ghost, I tell you. I shall not wear that surplice any more; some lost soul has stood next to it."

On the third or fourth night after, little Wladislav was again awakened.

"Softly," his father was saying; "go on tiptoe, so that they do not hear you, and catch me one of those little dwarfs."

"Little dwarfs!" echoed Wladislav, in

surprise. "I see no little dwarfs anywhere."

"Are you blind?" said his father, angrily. "Do you not see them clambering over the walls in thousands?"

Wladislav looked hard, and saw little shadows glancing up and down the room.

"They are no dwarfs, father," he said at length; "they are the leaves of the apple-tree flickering outside in the moonlight."

But the third vision which Father Stanislaus had he kept a secret; and indeed his little son would have found some difficulty in explaining that away. All at once the priest found himself pursued by a scowling face with a pair of wooden, staring eyes. He saw it upon the pages of his psalter; he saw it on the church steeple, usurping the place of the weathercock—indeed it was everywhere. The father had recourse to paroxysms of devotion, but that, instead of banishing it, made it only more obtrusive; and there it was, a veritable incubus that clung with iron talons to his prayers, and prevented them from flying up to heaven.

And yet when Father Stanislaus looked at the length and breadth of the thing, he found it was only what he had to expect. These visions, as a rule, emanated from the Tempter, who had been an important ingredient in most cases of authenticated sainthood. Evidently the father's attempts were becoming serious enough to call for interference, and that was in itself a partial acknowledgment of success. The worst of it was that this necessitated a division of devotional energy: one-half the prayers had to go for the removal of the unwelcome familiar, which meant so much time lost from the main object in view. But the strange thing was that day by day the uncanny presence became more evident; and though Father Stanislaus pressed his hands to his forehead till he nearly squeezed his eyes from their sockets, and though he swayed his body till it became lithe as an acrobat's, the hateful face, with its wooden, staring eyes, could not be shaken off. Nay, it waxed and expanded and eclipsed the horizon of his soul and senses. And if this went on, his prospect of saintdom would dwindle away to a peep-hole; and when that too had closed up there would be nothing but a dark infinity of scowling face, with two staring wooden eyes for constellations.

It was Pentecost morning, and Father Stanislaus had woke up with a bad headache; it was not exactly a headache, but his five senses seemed playing at leap-frog inside his head, and a rough-and-tumble crew they were. He had had another vision, and now he sat pensively at the side of his bed thinking it over. The scowling face aforementioned had interviewed him in his sleep and had suggested a compromise; not only that, but it had even specified the terms in an offhand manner, as though it did not wish to make a bargain. But Father Stanislaus remembered that there had been something in these terms to make him bate and haggle, that he had writhed in the grip of the cold, staring eyes that had clutched and grabbed till they had torn his heart out of him—at least, it could not be there any more, for in the night he had felt it ache very much when he had agreed to do what was asked of him; but now everything was void and blank. And somehow he felt glad of it, for thus it seemed he was escaping some great agony.

Little Wladislav, for his part, had passed a very good night, and now sat anxiously by the small kitchen oven watching the morning meal in preparation, and trying to persuade himself, with indifferent success, that he was not really so hungry as he felt. He always had to deal very diplomatically with his appetite in the mornings, because his father commenced the day by telling his beads for an hour or two. In the daytime it was not so bad; he could drop in on the neighbouring housewives and get a crust here and a saucer of milk there; but in the morning they were busy making the beds and getting the children ready for school, so that visitors were not encouraged. To-day, as it was a festival, he anticipated a longer wait, because his father commemorated such occasions by a double dose of devotion. So he was not a little surprised to hear him descend swiftly the creaky staircase and come straight across the sitting-room into the kitchen.

"Make haste and eat," were his first words. "We shall go over to Pirna, to bid your grandmother a merry holiday."

Wladislav looked up eagerly—it was too good to be believed. "To Pirna?" he repeated, to make sure his ears had not deceived him.

"Yes, to Pirna—why not to Pirna?" said his father, fretfully.

Wladislav had no objection; it was a grand thing to go to granny's. He had seen her only twice since they carried his mother away in the black box, for there had been no one to take him, and grandmother herself could not walk three steps without her crutches. So he needed no further bidding. He did not eat much, partly from excitement, and partly because he wished to keep himself hungry for the poppy-cake and dried apples which he knew were in store for him. In five minutes he was ready.

"Shall I put on my beaver cap and velvet doublet?" he asked, tugging eagerly at his father's girdle, for otherwise it was hard to attract his attention.

"There is no need," said the priest, glancing hurriedly away from the little face; "you will be as welcome in your workaday clothes."

Little Wladislav wondered; he knew grandmother would like to see him in all his finery, for she had said the last time, "When you come, always come spruce and smart, for then it will make me feel as though Anushka's hand had tended you." However, he said nothing, and nimbly followed his father into the street; but as they stepped over the threshold he looked up wistfully and said:

"The garden door is open; some one will come and steal my spade and pick-axe."

"You are a little fool! People do not thieve on holy-days."

Wladislav shrank back at the rough tone, and kept silent for fear of irritating his father, else the latter might change his mind and give up the excursion. So he ran on briskly to keep alongside of the priest's lanky strides.

"A merry holiday, your reverence—a merry holiday, little Wladislav," met them on every side.

"God's greeting to you,' shouted Wladislav, joyously, in reply; "we are going to Pirna—to Granny's." He felt so glad that he would have the whole world know his happiness; but he wondered why his father did not answer these good people. So he was twice as cordial to make up for his sullenness, for he loved his father, especially this morning, and he wanted folks to think well of him.

They had come to the first milestone, where the road branched. Wladislav was skipping on in front—he knew the way—when his father's voice stopped him.

"Follow to the left," he was saying across his shoulder, without looking back.

Wladislav stopped in perplexity. Granny lived on the road to the right; by the left, he knew, you came first to the pine forest, where the shadows lay thick even in the broadest daylight; further on there were ditches and a swamp, and beyond that probably lay the end of the world. What was the use of going there? The other road was quite straight and direct, and already from the second milestone could be seen Granny's cottage, looking like a chalk cliff in the dazzling glory of its whitewash, and blinking into the sunshine with half-closed shutters. But Wladislav had faith in his father, who, he was sure, could reach a place sooner by a round-about path than most people could by a straight one ; but then he was so much cleverer than everybody else. So he made his little legs as long as possible, breaking into a run till he had caught his father up. Soon the road on the right was lost to view, and the air grew strong and intoxicating with the heavy smell of the pinewood. The sun stopped reluctantly on the skirts of the forest, watching them enviously penetrate into the cool, dew-soaked glades. Little Wladislav took his father's hand, and as he touched it he felt it give a twitch as though it had been seared with hot iron ; nor did it close over his own hand with that reassuring grip he liked to feel on occasions when his heart beat as loud and as fast as it did now. And the greater the stillness, the louder grew the thumping noise in his chest ; he could not even look up to his father's face, for fear of tripping over the gnarled roots and amputated stumps. It had now got very still, till suddenly a clap of thunder broke on his ear—but no, it was only his father speaking.

"Little son," he said, "do you remember the time when I first taught you your letters?"

"Yes, father," gasped Wladislav, in wonder at the strange question and the strange tone.

"What was the story I first taught you to read?" went on the strange voice.

"It was about a wicked man Abraham, who would have slain his poor little Isaac—only God sent a ram instead," Wladislav answered pat. "It is wicked for people to kill their little sons, is it not, father?"

"Not when it is in the cause of God," came the answer, sullenly and tardily.

"More likely it would be the cause of the——" broke from Wladislav; but he stopped short in affright, and looked around him shrinkingly. He dared not utter the name amidst these desolate places—he did not know who might be listening behind the trees, and he wished they were at Granny's, where a crucifix hung on every wall.

"Let us go faster, father; we shall be late," he ended up with instead.

But for answer his father came suddenly to a standstill. What was the good of going farther? He could not get away from the dread task that lay before him, and why not get done with it here? Everything was so dark and gloomy, and the matter in hand needed no superabundance of light. And just then Wladislav looked up, saw the hard, glittering thing in his father's hand, and shrieked:

"What would you do with the knife, father?"

"I am going to play at Abraham, and you at Isaac," came the answer, almost sobbingly, from the priest's lips. "Nay, do not seek to escape, little son—you must die; I have promised it in the vision, for unless I sacrificed my dearest it would never leave me, and I could not become a saint. Quick! say a paternoster——"

"I shall not run away, father," whispered Wladislav, with trembling lips. "I was just peering through the trees if perchance the ram was there. Look, father—you are so tall—look hard through the trees. Has not God sent the ram?"

Father Stanislaus looked right and left, and on each side he was fenced in by a scowling face with staring, wooden eyes; and at the sight he felt the hard, glittering thing in his hand become alive, and it writhed and darted till it had forced its way into the soft flesh again and again.

And this was the Ascension of Father Stanislaus.

Granny sat all day at the window, looking out anxiously.

"If only Anushka were alive," she muttered, shaking her head sorrowfully.

OUT OF THE LAND OF BONDAGE

Though the mouth of the well in the passing of time
Be clogged by the clambering weeds as they climb,
Who knows but beneath, all undreamt-of, unseen,
Its waters as erstwhile leap limpid and clean?

"AN inn, you inquire for, good sir?—and that upon the eve of the Passover? How come you to be on your travelling during the festival?"

"I miscalculated the distance, for I thought to be at Vikulno ere dark."

"It's two hours further, and the roads are difficult; therefore come with me. The other masters of houses doubtless passed you by when they chose their strangers because you do not carry the air of a would-be guest, either in your aspect or in your garb; and thus you must be content with me."

"I thank you, but I need no charity,

and require no service without payment. I have set my heart on the inn."

"Then you must come with me perforce—there is no hostel in the town, so that travellers quarter with whoever receives them; and no one shall say that Nachemyah Turok showed unmindful of the precept concerning the stranger in the gate. Nor let us talk of money and payment upon a holy-day. Is this not the season when we say, 'This is the bread—he who is without, let him sit down and eat'?"

There could be no mistaking the cordiality with which the old man urged the younger to give him his company. The two were standing by the doorway of the synagogue, that was already wrapped in gloom, for the evening service was over and each man had hurried home to inaugurate the festival in the midst of his own.

"Let us not delay any longer," went on Nachemyah; "Hagar, my wife, will be anxious."

"Do not think me surly," said the stranger; "I would come gladly, but I do not care to witness the light of joyous faces and listen to their laughter. I prefer sitting in the abode of wayfarers like myself, where one knows not the other, and where sadness of mien and silence of speech concerns not your neighbour and affords no comment."

"Then you may rest assured," answered Nachemyah; "think not you are going to a house where there are many faces and much laughter. It is a house of solitude wherein dwell I and my wife Hagar; and if your heart is not in joyous mood it shall be not so much out of keeping with the rest. Let us go faster, pray; my house stands the last in the town, for—that thou mayest know it—I am the guardian of the graveyard."

And so the two walked on in silence.

"It is in no auspicious time that you have come to sojourn in these parts," said Nachemyah after a while. "There have arrived tidings that the hearts of the rulers are ill-affected towards our brethren, and there has been maltreatment and mishandling of them in places not so far hence. At Olnitzk they have burned the house of prayer, at Ramant they have pillaged the dwellings, and in other towns they have cast children and bedridden women into the streets at night-time. Nor is that the worst they have done—I will not defile my mouth with the utterance. Grant God the evil may not come nearer our own doors."

"I have seen the sights you speak of," said his companion, "and I did not care to look twice. But I have not come to sojourn here. Rarely it is that I make my stay long in any one place, for my heart is ever dragging me hither and thither so that I can find no resting-place. And it is chiefly at this time of the year that the feeling is strongest upon me, and I would wander to the ends of the earth, seeking a home and kith and kin. But one does not find them for the mere seeking— these things are in the hand of God."

"You are young to have lost all your kindred," said Nachemyah.

"I did not lose them—I do not remember when I had them to lose. I have abided amidst strangers—but what am I telling you? Your wife will scold you hard to have brought for her table-fellow a mouther of lamentations, and that on a festival when we should serve God by merriment."

They had come to the outskirts of the town, and Nachemyah pointed to the bright glittering windows of his house.

"I have brought thee a guest, Hagar," he said, entering; "one only, not two as thou didst ask me, so that for once we might have the full number for saying grace. But there were no others left; the rich have ever the preference of means to find favour in God's eyes—but let us be thankful for one."

"Blessed be your coming, my son," said the woman, and her glance was as kindly as her words. It did not happen too often that their lonely meal was shared by a third, and another face would give a more homely look to the dreary, straggling chamber. It would also make her feel bolder, for despite her long association with the burial-ground she still was a little afraid of it after dark. Each time she passed the window she could see it grinning at her with its long white teeth, for such, by a trick of her fancy, appeared to her the tombstones of gleaming chalk. And, again, she did not like the clattering sound that came from there on gusty nights like this one; of course she knew that it was only the rackety old wood-tablet with the mourner's blessing daubed on it, but it might—how could she tell?—be also the rattling of the skeletons in their coffins. But with the stranger's presence a wonderful assurance had come over her; for to-night at least she was certain that tombstones would be tombstones, and the crazy wooden board would bring no suggestion of the dead playing at skittles with their bones.

"Who are you, and whence come you?" she said. "Be not angry at my question; it is but courteous to inquire of the guest, lest he think he is asked to sit at table as though he were a stray dog of whose comings and goings no count is taken." And there was a softness in her words that made the stranger feel they were half a benediction.

"I have come lately from Biastotzk; but I am known in the parts beyond for an expounder of the Holy Writ, and my name is not unfamiliar to the ears of those that dwell there. Do not think me a braggart, but these things are such, and I cannot say otherwise."

"Nachemyah, in a good hour didst thou

go to the synagogue," said Hagar. "I doubt if any of the well-to-do of the town are honoured as we are this night, for the learned in the Law are the crown of Israel. Nachemyah, thou shalt be a king in good earnest this evening, for thou hast a crown in thy house. And at last my heart's desire is granted; long have I wished for such an one as you," and she turned to the stranger, "to make clear to me the difficult places of the Hagada that have harassed my mind these many years; and be not vexed if I pester you with many questions, but answer them. What name shall I give to you, my son?"

"Avromelya I am called," said the stranger, and a blush of modesty came over his face at Hagar's garrulous praise. And at the mention of his name he saw his host and hostess dart a quick glance at each other, and immediately the woman's face became drawn with pain.

And Nachemyah, as though to give a different turn to their thoughts, said, speaking very fast, " Long of tongue thou art, like all women—there thou standest prating of many things while our guest's heart may be aching with hunger and weariness; what manner of entertainment dost thou call this?"

At the rebuke Hagar cast down her eyes, and went quickly to the bedchamber to fetch the pillows whereon her husband was to recline like a king on his divan; for on this night every Hebrew is a sovereign in his house, and he may couch at table, leaning on his elbow in token of his freedom. Thus would he spite the Egyptian, who presumed to trammel him with the yoke of slavery, and Pharaoh no doubt would turn in his grave at the insult.

And then the ceremony went apace. Nachemyah consulted his patriarchal prayer-book for the regulations and ordinances that affect the arrangement of the various accessories of the paschal table. He had done so each Passover for thirty years past, and still he did not remember whether the roasted egg was to stand to the right or left of the heap of unleavened bread; and whether the bitter herbs had their place over or under the spice mixture that was the colour and stood for the emblem of the loam in which the children of Israel had worked. And the scorched mutton-bone, which, according to tradition, was there to make mockery of the Mizraim's worship of the beasts of the field, gave its usual deal of trouble in locating it. And at last everything stood in its place, and Nachemyah said, keeping his eyes on the page :

"Avromelya—if I may call you thus—you are the youngest of the party, do you ask the Question."

At that Avromelya seemed to remind himself of something. " Have ye no children ? " he asked. And it puzzled him a little to hear both husband and wife answer in the same breath and in the same tone :

" No, we are childless—God has given us no offspring."

And then the young man did as he was bidden, and began the recital of the catechism wherein, by question and answer, Israel repeats to itself the assurance of its deliverance, heedless of the bitter irony ; for where is the truth, where is the consummation of what it so triumphantly implies ? But form is form, be there reality or not. And so Avromelya read : " Why is this night different to all other nights ? " And as he dwelt on each word lovingly and reverently, Hagar watched his lips move, and a feeling came over her that she must reach out her arms and draw his head to her bosom. Nachemyah listened solemnly, and when it was finished he did not immediately follow on the cue with, " Slaves we were unto Pharaoh, until the Lord led us forth with a strong hand and an outstretched arm," but sat on dreaming, so that Avromelya looked up wonderingly at the silence, and Nachemyah fell to it shamefacedly, as though he had been detected in some misdoing. And then the two men read on quickly, because they remembered it all by heart, and Hagar dragged after them painfully, for the words were hard to spell, and her heart was full of other memories. Suddenly she stopped and lifted her head.

" Heard ye nothing ? " she said.

" No, I heard nothing—do not interrupt the reading," said Nachemyah, severely, and the droning of the voices went on. But after a minute or two Hagar leapt up with her hand to her heart.

" Heard ye not the strange hollow sound that comes floating from the streets ? " she asked, anxiously.

"I heard a low rumbling, but it is only a clod of earth rolling into an open grave," said Nachemyah, and looked reproof at her.

"I thought it came from the town side, not from the graveyard," ventured Avromelya; "and now indeed I can hear it more plainly, for my ears are younger than yours—a deep, confused hum, as of many voices in turmoil."

"Perhaps a fire has broken out," said Nachemyah.

"It cannot be, or we should have heard the tocsin boom," said Hagar.

But Avromelya rose up quietly, and going to the door he opened it. "There is no redness in the sky," he said across his shoulder. And then there surged in the subdued murmur of a multitude when it is swayed by a great emotion. And at last there could be no mistaking the sounds of lamentation and the cries of terror; for the tumult waxed and rose higher and higher. Avromelya came back still more quietly, and his face was very white.

"It is the rioters—the town is doomed," he said, under his breath.

But Hagar caught the words, and clasping her hands she gasped, "Oh, thou dear God, save us from destruction, and turn not Thy face from us in the hour of our peril! Nachemyah, quick, let me blow out the candles; it is lawful to do so even on a Sabbath when there is danger of life. In the darkness we may creep away and escape."

But Nachemyah sat there immovably, and at his wife's words he lifted his eyes to hers slowly.

"Art thou not ashamed," he said—"thou that makest pretence of so much piety in thy ways; art thou not ashamed to think thou couldst turn aside God's purpose by the quenching of a rushlight? And if our destiny is upon us, shall it reach us less surely because we shirk it in the shadow of the darkness? Sit down, and rather thank God that our abode is at a distance from the others, for thus we shall have time to finish the service of the night. Where did we leave off, Avromelya? Unless"—and the thought came to him suddenly—"you wish to escape betimes; for what is our peril to you? Therefore go your way."

"Like a sheep that runs from the flock

because the shearer is coming?" said Avromelya. "But how can you tell? I am a stranger to you, and you have no knowledge of my nature. I shall stay — to the end. Let us read on."

And then the two men continued with flying breath, while Hagar sat shaking and listening as though every pore of her body were an ear. And the uproar came nearer and nearer, till they could distinguish single voices.

"That was Lesser Sundra's shout; they must be doing him some hurt, or he would not bellow thus like a bull," moaned Hagar, tremblingly. "Oh! what will become of us?"

The two men made no answer; they had come to the pouring out of the fourth glass of wine according to the prescribed number, and, after one or two attempts, Nachemyah handed the bottle to Avromelya, saying:

"Do you the pouring—your sinews are stronger than mine." And now they had come to the tale of the lamb that was bought for six groats, which traces the history of Israel through the list of his persecutors right up to the hands of God, the avenger; and as the last words were uttered there came the stamping of heavy footsteps, and with a thud the door fell splintered from its hinges. Hagar buried her face in her hands, and the two men stood gazing wild-eyed at the comers. And as they sprang into the room, beetle-browed, straggling-haired, sheepskin cap and all, they could hardly be called a pretty sight. They were mujiks—peasants—all the three of them, and they had been asked to lend a hand in the work of the night; and to the mujik no work is so much a labour of love as a Jews' hunt. But, whatever else it had been in their mind to do, no sooner had they entered, when they stopped short, and, stepping back a pace or two, gave a long, lingering stare at Avromelya. And for a moment there was a silence of death in the chamber; but then the intruders turned to one another and burst into a laugh, like the laugh of men who have been frightened by a shadow and laugh themselves to shame for their folly.

"Didst thou not think my thought, Karol?" said the first. "Thy thought was: 'We left him but an instant ago, and here he stands facing us.'"

"Be careful, Stephan," said the other. "Go not too near; it may be the Fiend. Nothing is impossible with these cursed Jew-folk; there is no reason why the devil should not come to visit them, and why the devil should not look like a commissioner of police. But we shall soon see."

And he stretched out his arms in the manner of a cross, while the others did likewise, and advanced straight on Avromelya, who did not know what to make of it.

"He has stood the test," said Stephan, "and therefore he cannot be the Evil One, and we have wasted a reverence. Ought it not to be that a Jew should fall dead each time one makes the sign of the cross?" And then, turning to those at the table, he went on, "Why do you stand there gaping, you god-slaying heretics? Why do you not thank Providence that has sent you three true believers to make vain your wicked rites and incantations, so that you lay up for yourselves less torment in hell?"

And striding up to the table, he surveyed the eatables on it.

"Look at the provision they have made for their honoured visitors," he jeered; "and that in return for the glad tidings we bring—may no one bring them better to the day of their death. Well, I am going to have my supper while we wait for the commissioner." And with one blow he sent Hagar staggering to the other end of the room, and seated himself in her place. The other two peasants stood looking on, laughing at Stephan's antics.

"No, I will not eat of your dishes; there may be poison in them, or human blood at the least. Here is honest Christian food." And from his knapsack he took a loaf of barley bread and a hunch of swine flesh, and laid them on the platter; and Hagar, as she saw it, wrung her hands at the defilement and Nachemyah ground his teeth in impotence. And while Stephan was eating, Karol and the other one came up, and Karol took one of the unleavened cakes; and as he bit into it he made a wry mouth, and spat the morsel upon the floor.

OUT OF THE LAND OF BONDAGE 159

"And this is what you feed on, you mongrels?" he cried. "Baked sawdust, into which you have been too niggardly to put salt. Poor creatures! Say, Stephan, would it not be true charity to give them some of that excellent Ruzzavana bread of thine, lest their souls should go out of them with their self-castigation?"

"Thou hast reminded me well," said Stephan, jumping up; and, cutting a slice from his loaf, he went up to Nachemyah, who cowered back and lifted his tunic over his head at the ruffian's coming. But Stephan rudely gripped it, so that it was torn down to the middle; and, forcing down the old man's arm, he held the forbidden leaven before his face. And Hagar shrieked aloud, as she saw Nachemyah's struggles and heard his agonised wail, "Have mercy on me!—kill me!—but do not make me transgress the commandment."

But Avromelya, who had stood there chafing all the time, could bear it no longer, and seizing Stephan with tight grip, he hurled him upon his haunches into the middle of the room. At that the other two rushed upon him and bore him down; and when Stephan had gathered himself up again he came and knelt on Avromelya's chest, clutching his neck with both his hands. But that did not suffice him; so, looking about the room, he saw an iron tripod in the corner, and when Karol had handed it to him he set it down with the bottom uppermost, so that its feet stood out like prongs, and crashed Avromelya's head against it heavily; and the tripod made a good battering-block, for it was harder than the flooring, which was of caked turf. And no one could tell what would eventually have become of Avromelya's head, had not the ring of spurs been heard outside and Karol had dragged his comrade forcibly from off his victim.

"Have done—the commissioner comes," he whispered.

And no sooner had Stephan got to his feet than there stepped into the room a man, young in years, but upon whose forehead were written large command and authority; and as he cast his eyes about and saw the signs of the commotion, he said sternly:

"There has been violence here; did I

OUT OF THE LAND OF BONDAGE

not tell you no one should be touched unless resistance was offered?"

"They did resist," said Stephan, sullenly. "I would give the old man of my bread, to make him strong for his pilgrimage, and then the young one here came and laid violent hands on me, your honour's servant; and for that I have chastised him."

And only then the new-comer became aware of the prostrate form of Avromelya where he lay half stunned. So, going over to him, he shook him by the shoulder.

"Get up, my good fellow; this is no time for lying at thy ease. Thou hast a long journey before thee, for thou and all thy folks must leave this town within the hour, and there is no escape. The rescript has arrived." Here he suddenly stopped short, and, bending low, he scanned Avromelya's features closely.

"By the clank of my scabbard," he cried, straightening himself, "this is wonderful!" And he took one of the candles from the table and held it close to the still face.

"It is indeed wonderful," said Karol, coming to his side; "the Jew-dog has stolen your honour's face, and will sneak into heaven pretending he is you. These Jews would cheat God Himself if they could."

But the commissioner was still standing in wonder; and indeed it was a thing to marvel at to see how the two men were like to one another, feature by feature and line by line.

"The Jew has fainted," he said; "give me some wine for him." And at the same time he began to unfasten Avromelya's doublet. And when he saw Stephan's finger-marks on the throat, he said, angrily: "You have throttled him between you—curses on your murderous hands." For he felt as if he saw his own corpse lying before him. But just then Avromelya gave a little gasp and opened his eyes; and just then, too, the commissioner caught sight of the string of catgut that was tied round his neck, and to the catgut there hung an onyx stone, pure of colour and oblong of shape. And at view of it he lifted his hands to his forehead, for he felt the sweat starting upon it.

"I cannot understand this," he said, half aloud. "This is yet more wonderful.

The very thing I have been looking for, and here I find it about the neck of a Jew. My good fellow, I am no robber; thou must give me this, and I will give thee its value in money. For it matches mine, and Fanushka, my little mistress, has been harassing me into grey hairs to find her another for a pair of pendants. Give it to me; the money will come thee in good stead on thy journey."

Stephan and Karol looked on in angry surprise. Bandy words with a Jew? That was setting a bad example. The Jew was the common quarry of everybody, to despoil at pleasure; the idea of compensation was absurd. But they looked at the commissioner and kept their thoughts to themselves.

Avromelya held tight to the trinket with all the strength of his feeble hand, and murmured, " Do not take it from me, good sir. Have compassion; it is what I hold dearest of all the world. It is to me the memory of a home I never knew, of parents whose face I have never kissed, and upon it I set all my hope of happiness that is to befall me. Take whatever else I possess, though I am a poor man, but leave me this that is at once my poverty and my wealth.

All during this Hagar had crouched in her corner listening eagerly to the talk of the men; but she understood little of it, for they spoke in Russian. Then by the flash of the candlelight she saw the agate round Avromelya's neck, and at the sight a flash of mingled joy and terror glanced through her heart. And, stealthily creeping up to where he lay, she flung herself upon him, and, taking the stone in her hands, she cried, wildly:

"Oh, to think that my prayers and midnight weepings have been of avail! Thou hast then come back to me after many years of waiting, O my—— But let me talk and tell thee everything, so that, hearing, thou mayest believe." And then her speech flowed forth in a cataract of words. "Many years ago I had two children that were born within the same hour, and the face of one was the face of the other, like and similar as are the stars of heaven. And lest the two should be confounded and we should forget who is the eldest, so that he might observe the fast of the firstborn and be the first to be called up to the reading of the Law, I took two agate stones that my mother gave me from her necklet; and on one I had engraved the letter Aleph and on the second the letter Beth, and hung the first round the neck of the elder and the second round the younger. And look if it is not as I speak—here is the Aleph upon the stone. And when they were six years old God was angry with us, and took away our children. For it was upon the day preceding the Passover, when Nachemyah had gone across country, and I had run to the burning-place to burn the leaven-offering — the ladle and the bread-crumbs and the candle and the feather; and I had left the little ones playing outside the door. And when I returned and looked for them they had vanished. Then I ran weeping to the neighbours, and they told me that a pair of Cossacks had passed through the town in the direction of my house. And then I knew my fate; and presently the town shepherd came to me and said he had seen my two children, each on the saddle of one rider, and that when they had come to the crossway the two had separated, and the one rider went one way and his fellow the other. And the name of the elder child was Avromelya, like thine. And all this is true as the Word of God. Oh, Nachemyah! why dost thou stand mute, like a block of stone? Why dost thou not speak and bear me out, and protest and swear by thy life in the World-to-come that this is as I have said?"

But Nachemyah had been standing all the while staring blankly from Avromelya to the commissioner, and when he beheld the agate his senses turned like a whirlpool.

"Why should I swear, Hagar?" he said at last. "If all thy tokens bring no belief to his heart, and if the voice of his mother as she soothed him to sleep with her lullaby ring not in his ears, what can I, even I, say to convince him?"

"But I would be convinced—I would believe gladly," said Avromelya, eagerly; "and yet why did you tell me before, when I asked, that you had been ever childless?"

"It was the vow we had taken to one another," said Hagar, "never to speak

OUT OF THE LAND OF BONDAGE 167

of our children that were, and to make belief that God had given us none; for our two hearts were breaking with the woe, and if the heart of one broke before the other, what would be the life of the one remaining?"

Then Avromelya sat himself up, and said thoughtfully: "This is what I remember, how I came to the house of a teacher of the Law—a solitary man. And I abided with him, and he called me son and I called him father. But on his deathbed he told me that he had found me by the roadside, and had brought me up for his own; and he urged me to go and seek my parents, and to hold by the amulet because it might serve for a recognition. And that is why I wander, not finding rest anywhere, and why ever at this season of the year my feet have wings and cannot abide in one place. Am I not to believe you? Am I not to believe my own heart, that has cast forth its demon of unrest ever since I entered this dwelling? Come—father, mother—come!" And he stretched out an arm about each, and their heads and lips were close together.

The commissioner stood looking on and

wondered. He could not make out how it was that he, a true Slav of purest race, who spoke the language of the country and none other, should understand the strange talk of these strange people. And yet of all that had been said not a word had escaped his comprehension. A son had strayed back to the house of his parents, and the mother had set aside all doubt by her story. What was that recollection from the buried past that had made him understand? What was the instinct that had haunted him all his life, and the dim uncertainty that had made him so often clench his hands in his hopeless search for light and clearness? Perhaps here was the revelation Long, long ago he remembered certain people had asked him a certain question, and he had answered "Naphtali." And then they had beaten him, and told him that he was to answer "Kyriloff," not "Naphtali"; and how he had lain awake at night repeating the name, lest he should answer "Naphtali" when he was questioned and be beaten again. Here he was—Ivan Kyriloff; but what had become of the Naphtali? The memory of the name clung to him and came as a voice from another life. These people here had bred great prophets in their race, and perhaps they would tell him.

"Wait for me outside, and do not enter before I call you," he said to the three myrmidons, who had eyed the scene in blank amazement. And when the door had closed behind them, he said (and his lips shaped themselves unconsciously to the strange tongue he had just heard):

"What means Naphtali?"

At the question Hagar turned round, and only then and for the first time she saw the likeness; and when she heard the name she turned white, and would have fallen but for Avromelya's arm.

"Naphtali means my second son," she gasped; and then an inspiration came over her—the inspiration of every mother, brute or human, and pointing to him solemnly, she said: "Thou art he—God has told me." And at the answer the questioner took a step forward, and bowed his head as though he would ask for her blessing. And suddenly he put his hand in his pocket and took out the agate, which he had possessed he could not remember how long; and he thought of the unaccountable jealousy he had felt each time Fanushka's dainty fingers had toyed with it, and the puzzled perplexity each time she had asked him the meaning of the mystic symbol scratched upon it. But now he could read it quite easily—it was Beth, the letter shaped like a house; and here they stood before him, his flesh and blood, his father, mother, and twin-brother, the living voices that had called to him from the dead past. And without stood the ruthless horde that was to uproot them from the soil of their birth and drive them homeless out into the unknown wilderness; and he could do nothing. But no, he could do a great deal.

"Will you take me for your son and brother?" he asked, with glistening eyes. "Will you take me, the apostate, the baptised, who has grown up among your adversaries and has hated you with their hatred? You shall teach me again your ways that I have forgotten, and I shall share with you through good and evil—only do not make me an outcast for ever."

There was a long silence, and then Nachemyah went and took his outstretched hand; and looking hungrily into his eyes, he said:

"My son thou art, wert, and shalt be evermore, although all the sins of Satan be fastened upon thy head. But bethink thee—what couldst thou not do if thou wert to remain here among thy suffering brothers and in a little way avert their evils? Is it not more fitting thou shouldst stay here and be their shield?"

But Naphtali shook his head, and said, mournfully: "No, I could not stay here knowing what I know, and seeing what I see; for my heart might bleed itself to death at the sight, and when it is dead I should be pitiless like the rest—save them from me, and me from myself."

"Then come, in God's name," said Nachemyah.

Naphtali went to the door, and opening it, he told the men outside: "You need wait no longer; go and help the others, but tell them upon their lives to deal gently. As for me, I shall convey these people to Vikulno—to the ecclesiastic court, for the woman has accused the men of unholy rites—they shall be my charge.'

And when he had watched them out of sight he came back.

"Quickly," he said, "get together whatever you may carry in your hands; and here I have a blank passport that will give us unconditional passage wherever we go. At Vikulno I shall claim from the bankers the three thousand roubles of my savings to furnish us for our journey; and for the rest, I and Avromelya have two pair of strong arms to keep us all from want—and God will help. And now come —let us go to the countries across the sea where there is liberty and where men do not rend their fellows from narrowness of heart. Come, father, mother, brother— let us go hence, out of the land of bondage!"

RABBI ELCHANAN'S QUEST

THE words of Rabbi Elchanan, the son of Aaron the Levite, unto Riffka, daughter of Baruch the Scribe:—

Peace and greeting unto thee, oh bride of my youth, mainstay of my manhood, comforter of my old age. Whereas Leyb Tchariner thy kinsman has handed to me a letter written at thy dictate and over thy name—for thou art thyself no expert in penmanship, despite the cunning of thy father—what says the proverb? "The children of shoemakers go barefoot"—the letter, wherein thou inquirest concerning me and makest great lamentation that since the day I set foot from our threshold no tidings have reached thee of my wellbeing. And at sight and perusal thereof my soul lifted her hands in repentance. For as thou sayest, it is truly spoken: seven portions of the Law have been read, and on the coming Sabbath shall be uttered the third Benediction of the New Moon since what time I started forth to sojourn amongst strangers; the cause thereof being, as thou well knowest, the gathering of a marriage-portion for our daughter, the sole and single issue of our love—may God make her like unto Sarah, Rachel and Leah, her forbears. And verily, were it not for that, I should have returned long ere this, for one endures hardship and tribulation in dwelling among men of alien speech and customs. But the matter proceeds somewhat tardily, and it is because my mind is ever intent upon the achieving thereof that my hand has been turned aside from the admonishings of my heart. Now, however, open thine ears unto the tale of my wanderings; for it shall be set forth in all detail, both my pilgrimage and all that appertains unto my quest.

It was upon the third day after Pentecost, if my memory serves me truly, that I girded up my aged loins to make adventure into the land of Britannia, whereof, as report says with truth, a woman is the ruler, a land lying towards the sinking of the sun. And further I remember how my going forth laid a gloom upon thy soul, and how thou didst endeavour vainly to clutch me by the caftan and hold me back with much shrieking and wringing of hands, until the women surrounded thee and conveyed thee to thy couch, whereon thou didst lie, a swoon holding thy senses captive. And as I turned me and gazed back, behold, methought that my house—to compare small things to great—seemed likest to Yerusholayim upon the day of its destruction. But wherefore didst thou afflict thy soul? Knowest thou not that God is ever at the right hand of the righteous and maketh clear his path from the ambushes of wicked men? And further, was there not a dire stress upon me to collect the amount of the dowry? For I am a man, poor after God's own heart, as the saying goes, and the poor must make trial of many things before they enter the palace of happiness, and then it is mostly through a postern-gate. With these thoughts did I set out; and many men of the congregation remitted their toil in their several handicrafts to give me escort as far as Kavass-Novrod, where there was to await me, according to concert, a driver with his conveyance to carry me across the frontier for a consideration. But when we came up, he made show of being very wroth, and looked very angry as to his eyes, saying that for my account he had delayed long over the given time, and that he would incur much blame and abuse from his master on his return. And upon that plea he made claim that the stipulated hire must be increased by fifty copecks. And what could I do, being in the hands of the Philistine and oppressed by him? And thereupon we drove off, and the company followed three ells shouting after me the usual "May the Lord bless thee and preserve thee," repeating it seven times. Then indeed my heart became desolate and I wept many tears; and for a distraction I took from my wallet "The Guide of the Ignorant," and read therein until it came on dark and my eyes refused their service. Then I laid me down and slept throughout the night without a fear, for I had prayed my night prayer and had dealt with the Tetragrammaton by Gematrya, so as to conjure Michael and Gabriel to stand by and encompass me with their wings. And towards dawn, when all the stars had returned to heaven for the morning prayers, the bal-ha-golah, the driver to wit, awakened me by a thrust of his foot.

"Rouse thee," he cried, "and get thee into thy hiding-place; for we have passed the last milestone before the toll-house."

Now I must make known to thee, oh wife of my bosom, that the waggon whereon I rode was freighted with skins of bullocks; and my plan was to conceal myself amongst these, and under cover thereof to cross the frontier. For not being possessed of a passport, since I was lacking the money wherewith to procure such an one, necessity was upon me to pass over the border by stealth; and thus is a poor man rendered dishonest in the land of oppression. Now as to the bullock-skins, they were but freshly hided, so that they lay limp and huddled, and the smell was not the savour of spice and cinnamon. Into these, then, I coiled myself, and the driver heaped them about my feet and body that I might not be discovered.

So we rode on, I direly struggling with my breath, until I heard a voice cry "Halt!" And then indeed my gizzard quaked mightily within me.

"What kind of manure dost thou cart there, Gregorov?" asked one of the sentries; for I could hear the clanking of their sabres.

"No manure," answered the driver; "untanned leather, that is all."

"And how much carcase inside?" spoke the sentry.

"By the head of my patron saint," said the driver, "no living thing could draw breath in there, unless it be a snoutless skunk."

"Or a Jew," added the sentry, and they all laughed inordinately.

So we were allowed to pass, and I crept from underneath my cover and eagerly quaffed the air of heaven. And then the driver importuned me strongly to give him yet two more roubles for the danger he had run; or else he would turn back to the custom-house and deliver me up. But I prevailed upon him to wait till we reached an inn, for I was at that moment at my devotions and might not engage in business of any sort. And no sooner had we come to the inn, when I plied him with vodka—the cheap kind at two copecks the measure; and he being weary with night-vigil and drinking upon an empty stomach, became drowsy and incontinently he slept. And thereupon I debated with myself as to the two roubles I had promised him. Not that I had intention to withhold them from him in requital for his greed, nor did I think of the kick which he had bestowed upon me; but there came into my mind the saying of our sages: "Whoso awakeneth a sleeper, draggeth a human soul out of heaven by the feet." So, not wishing to commit iniquity, and not knowing how long his drunken sleep might endure, being myself in haste, I waited not to hand him the money, but got me forth. And that is how I slipped under the hands of the frontier-watchmen; for God had stricken them with blindness.

And now I had come into the land of Ashkanaz, which is Edom on the hither side of Jordan, forasmuch as its people are evilly-minded towards our race. And I made observation that their language is not unlike our own, being, in fact, an abortion thereof, and comparable to it in the degree of similitude between an ape and a man; and they speak it with much mincing of the mouth, even like girls when they are about to be kissed on the lips. But of that I have no knowledge, and speak only upon report and hearsay. So being now, as it were, in the wilderness, I followed closely upon the instructions which Moshke Kitsler, the glazier, had imparted unto me. For thou knowest the story how he went to this country of Britannia two years ago, having received a letter to come and claim his brother's inheritance; and when he arrived, behold there had been no brother, and there was no inheritance, and the whole thing was the chicanery of some one who bore Moshke a grudge—suspicion pointing to Elya Schmendriak, who had gone to this town of London because Moshke had married the woman whom Elya had loved. And I have sought out Schmendriak, and questioned him straightly upon the matter; but he looked at me with brazen eyes and denied all knowledge of it. So then I went by the instruction which Moshke has bought at great cost and by much tribulation of soul.

And first he had enjoined me to make my way to Ostrovno; and since there was a market gathering at the place on the morrow, I had no trouble in finding accommodation with one of the waggoners, of whom there were many proceeding thither. And by reason of one of the horses falling lame, we arrived not there till nightfall. Thenceforward I was to journey by a certain wondrous contrivance whereof I have heard men speak, but such as is unknown to thee that hast no concern in the business of the world. And though I have become familiar with the thing, and have used it for my service on several occasions by this time, the first sight and aspect of it brought upon me a deep amazement. For standing there in the gloom, having first converted much shining silver into a worthless four-cornered scrap of paste-paper, I thought I beheld a monster with fiery eyes issuing from the bowels of the earth, and flying towards me on wings of smoke and flame, uttering hoarse screeches from outspread jaws. And in these jaws, wherefrom upleapt long tongues of fire, I saw three men writhing like Chananya, Meshual and Azariah, in Nebuchadnezzar's furnace; yet, like them, they were not consumed. And then the prodigy stood still, panting and snorting, and I repeated the blessing which is incumbent upon us at beholding an untoward spectacle; but though I looked narrowly, I saw nothing of the two-score demons which Moshke swore were harnessed to the contrivance to set it in motion. And I could make no conjecture as to the mode of its propelling, but I stood and marvelled much at the cunning of the Gentile and his handiwork. And to me, thus distracted, there came a man, a dignitary of the town it seemed, for there were strings of golden braid across his bosom and a silver cockade in his cap.

"Where are you bound for?" he accosted me.

"I am going to Hamburg, to sail by the ship, your honour," I said.

"Then make haste and enter, else you will be left behind," he said, surlily. And with that he tore open a panel in the flank of the monster and flung me into the bulk and belly thereof; and its entrails were made of wood, fashioned into seats for men to sit upon. And for a little time I cowered there bewildered, for I felt the ground moving under me, and the darkness without whirled past me in great flakes of blackness, and there was no resting-place for my eyes. But when I turned them upon the company that sat by my side or fronting me, I saw much laughter upon their faces, whereat I was greatly comforted, for men do not smile when the danger of death is upon them. And among them there was a young man with glasses as to his eyes, a great scar as to his forehead, and a large pipe with long wooden stem and porcelain bowl as to his mouth. And he, having toised me for some time, addressed me as follows:

"What takes thee from out thy door-posts, Judas Yeshariat? Art thou going in search of the Lost Tribes?"

Thereon I made reply, swallowing my anger for that he had misnamed me strangely:

"My son, truly say our sages: 'he that openeth his mouth in ignorance, shall close it in confusion.' For it stands written that the Sons of Moses abide on the further side of the sand-river Sambatyon, and no man may cross it, for all the week it heaves with whirlwinds of stones and dust, and on the Sabbath, when it is at rest, it is not lawful to travel more than a thousand cubits; but the river measures a thousand and one.'

And the company listened with open ears; but the young man aforesaid, not heeding my presence, as though I were a haystack or a piece of rock, turned to them and said again:

"Is it not strange that these people cleave so perversely to their superstitions? And then there is much talk of progress and enlightenment in these days."

But then I could contain myself no longer, and burst into speech. "Young sir," I said, "it may be true that we are dark as to our beliefs, and that we do not see clearly the drift and purport of things; and that perchance may be because our eyes are blinded by tears for our nation's sorrows. But this much we know well amongst us, that it is enjoined to treat the stranger in our gates with kindness and courtesy, and that it is becoming for mere striplings to pay reverence unto grey hairs. For what blessing is there in knowledge if it be poisoned by malice of the heart?"

And then I ceased; but no one answered, and the young man busied himself strenuously in the rubbing of his spectacles. But I stood up and silently repeated the evening prayer, not forgetting the three backward paces at conclusion of the Eighteen Benedictions. And I slept soundly through the night; but in the morning, when I awoke, lo, a woe and a calamity had come upon me. For the ringlets at the side of my head, the glory of my temples and the badge of my piety, had been shorn away to the roots; and in my girdle was stuck a fragment of paper whereon were written these words—for I have had them expounded to me since: "Ahasuerus, thou hast convinced me of the error of my ways; therefore, mindful of what thou didst say, I have taken away with me thy grey hairs to reverence them at my leisure"; and the message was signed "Bierbauch, Student of the Theologies." And then I stood up, for I was left alone of all the company, and invoked upon him all the tribulations of Hiob, and all the imprecations which Balaam was not permitted to utter against the children of Israel, all these I flung forth against him;

and I doubt not that by this time his hands have been stricken with palsy and the sight has gone forth from his eyes. But as to my ringlets, even now they have not grown to their wonted length, and I fear me they will never again sprout with their ancient vigour, for I am an old man, and the marrow in my bones is dried up, and my sinews are brittle like stalks of straw. But I will refrain from overmuch lamentation; for it may betide that this missive reaches thee on a Sabbath, and it would be a sin on my head to move thy heart to sorrow on such a day. Rather will I go on to narrate what things further befell me ere that I reached my appointed goal; and in all my doings I followed the admonishings of Moshke, the glazier.

So when I came to Hamburg, which was the place of my embarkation, I wended my steps straightway to the ship; and as I was setting foot on the gangway, some one tapped me on the shoulder and said a quaint thing.

"Friend," he said, "thy Ten Commandments are dangling out behind thy back." And when I looked round it appeared that the fringes of my Four-corner Garment were overlapping the nape of my neck. And I bestowed them in their proper place, laughing much at the folly and ignorance of the Gentile. Then I passed on into the hollow of the ship, and they showed me a place where I was to abide during the voyage; it was dark and squalid, fitted with narrow wooden chests along the wall that looked like coffins: and I spat out in deprecation of the thought. But I was sorely afraid, for, as thou knowest, this was my first adventure by sea. Presently I heard a loud booming sound, that might have been the bellowing of sea-monsters; and soon after the ship gathered itself up and moved with a swinging motion from side to side. And first it swung not more violently than thou didst rock the cradle of our daughter Leah when she was yet a suckling; but soon it staggered, seemingly going two different ways at one time, until it overleapt its balance, and turned round and round upon itself, like a sleeper who is tossed by evil dreams at night, so that its flooring stood uppermost And then I sat down upon my wallet, for my bowels heaved and my gall-bladder crept up into my throat. And I will give thee a token of the feeling that came over me. For dost thou remember how thou didst go with the other folks of the town to witness the hanging of the prisoners that were taken in the time of the rebellion; and how there was a spell upon thine eyes, so that thou couldst not turn them away from the sight till the hanging was finished, and the six of them swung dead and stark? And then thou didst fall to the ground in a swoon, and for three days no food passed thy lips, and for three days thou didst vomit and retch, till I thought thou wouldst cast forth thy very soul. Of such a sort were my own sufferings during those days; and when I was reviving and began to feel I was still a living man, on the fourth night a storm arose that took the ship in its strong arms and flung it against the vault of heaven or thrust it into the caverns of the deep. And in my great fear I took my Pentateuch, and opened it, and upon its pages I sprinkled for a charm of the clean salt whereof I had taken with me a supply, so that I might not purchase of the Gentile, and I repeated psalms in multitude, and especially that which says: "They that go down in ships to the great waters, see the wonders of the Lord." For what death is there so horrible as to be devoured by the leviathans of the sea? And bitterly I regretted my improvidence in that I had not stocked myself with a sack of Sacred Earth that is dug from the soil of Palestine. For how else was I to find my way into the land of Canaan so it pleased God to put an end to my days? But it seemed that on the Day of Atonement my name had not been blotted out from the Book of Life, so that I survived; for after a while the sea made its peace with God, and the lightnings were quenched and the chariots of the thunder were again fastened to their staples. However, nothing further betided till we ran into harbour; but I vow upon my life and health, not less glad was I to leave the hollow of that ship than was Jonah when the whalefish spat him forth and he went to make prophecy unto the people of Nineveh.

Yet it concerned me somewhat to note that the day of my arrival was the second of the week, even the day whereon our sages say God created the Gehennom and Lilith and all the children of evil; and perchance it may be for that cause that my errand has not sped according to my desire. And having gone on land, I was even like unto the idols of the heathen, for I had eyes and saw not, and ears and heard not; and I was stricken as to the understanding of all things around me. But I chanced against a man of our own race and tongue, who proffered me his guidance unto the place of my destination. But he premised that it was necessary I should give him a piece of gold the equivalent of ten roubles, not for his own especial use and benefit, but because he affirmed it was the custom of strangers that arrived to bestow that sum upon the institutions for the tending of the sick and the study of the Sacred Writ. And I gave it, though with much secret doubtings of heart, and he conducted me faithfully. But upon inquiry I learned that there was no such custom, and that the man had deceived me. Now if he be in good earnest a Student of the Law, I grudge him not the money; but if he be not, may it go towards the healing of deadly sickness in his household.

So then I came to Leyb Tchariner, the

aforesaid, the kinsman ; and beneath his roof I tarried two days and two nights, until the stiffness had departed from out my limbs and I was rested. Then he went out, and on my behalf he hired a place of abode ; for he himself was greatly straitened as to room, dwelling as he did in three chambers with his wife and four sons and three daughters. And here I may note what thou wilt apprehend with wonder, even as I marvelled at the thing. For he has turned himself, for the earning of his bread, unto the making of shoes and other footgear, he that in his native country followed the calling of corn and wheat broker. But lest thou shouldst feel grieved thereat, be it known to thee herewith that in this country the constructing of shoes and garments is not deemed an indignity as it is with us, but that the makers thereof are not considered inferior to the scribes of books or to the keepers of taverns ; and many of them, and justly so, are advanced to posts of high honour in the community. And further I have here encountered sundry of my countrymen whom I never thought to set eyes upon before the resurrection of the dead ;

chiefly there was Chayim, the bellows-maker and tinker, who, as thou well knowest, disappeared from our township during the days that followed the conclusion of the Postanye, the revolution to wit. And we all thought that he had been conveyed to Siberia and had there died by reason of his sufferings. And the manner of his escape was as a miracle of God; for he was just about to issue from his house, having it in his heart to flee the country because of the suspicion attaching to him; and on the last step of his threshold there suddenly came into his path two emissaries of police. And one of them asked: "Art thou Chayim Drontovar?" for they knew him not by person. And then God breathed cunning and wisdom in his head so that he made reply: "No, I am not he; but I left him this instant at his midday meal with his family, and he dwells on the third flooring." And then they detained him no longer, and he lay hidden all during the day in a heap of refuse, and at night he escaped and came to this land. And his wife Mariam, even she who was flogged naked in the market-place to make her divulge her husband's secret resort, came at his bidding to this country after she had recovered from the effect of the scourging; but she has now departed this life, and the day whereon I met Chayim was the second anniversary of her death. And of one other I shall give thee tidings, though he is not worthy that his name be mentioned by mouths that utter words of righteousness; I speak of Lutke, the glutton as he was called. I doubt not thou rememberest him, a wild, dissolute fellow that had no shame in the sight of God or man; and a marvel it is that because of his deeds of evil and darkness the sun became not blotted out in the heavens. And finally, having filled full the measure of iniquity, and being in great straits for money, he went to the leader of the Attrat, the reconnoiterers, that made search in the forests for the insurgents hidden there—for this too happened in the time of the rebellion—and offered upon payment to show a place where was concealed great store of powder and shot and much accoutrement. And having received faithful promises of reward, he betrayed the spot, and according to his word was found much ammunition, which was carted away to Wratislavik, so that the insurgents were crippled of supplies and could not carry on the war in that part of the country. And he, to escape their wrath—for they would have flayed him alive—went back with the Attrat and sojourned among the soldiers; and thy sister's daughter has told me how she saw him go past her door unto the soldiers' mess and filled his bucket at the common cauldron with the rest. And one day he vanished; but the manner of my encountering him I shall relate anon.

In this place I shall make utterance of certain things that have come within my observation and have filled my heart with sorrow. For the people of our race dwelling in this country are for the most part of them by no means God-fearing. Rather do they offend greatly against the ordinances of our wise men. Thus it is that few of the women, though they be mothers of many children, wear the periwig which is the sign of matronhood; so that they walk abroad with outstretched necks and great luxuriance of hair-growth. And again the young men, and many of the elder too, shave the hair of the face and go about smooth like hounds that suffer with mange. Furthermore do they shamelessly carry rain-screens upon Sabbaths and festivals, though this is a city that has no fortifications but lies open to the country upon all four sides. But more than this : they wear garments wherein wool and cotton are intermingled — a heinous sin, and one for which there is no forgiveness. Yet this is not all; for I have heard of an abomination that is greater than the sum and aggregate of all the others. There is here a House of Prayer, rather should I call it a House of Blasphemy, where youths and maidens are gathered indiscriminately for the chanting of hymns on the Sabbath, and where a man makes music by breathing into long tubes of iron, and the destruction of our Sacred City is in no wise remembered amongst these people. And having been made aware of these things, straightway I eschewed also the drinking of milk, for in the eating of flesh I have not indulged since I left home. For in a land where such desecration is tolerated, no man is to be trusted for the purity and fitness of food. And ever since I have subsisted on the produce of the soil and of trees and upon the meat of fish roasted in oil, according to the manner and custom of the country.

And now touching the matter of the dowry. And upon this point I bear no grudge against him whom we have destined for our daughter's husband—though he has rated himself highly, even at the worth and value of five hundred roubles to be given for a marriage-portion. For he is a goodly youth, and master of a handicraft; nor shall it be with us as it is with many, to whom their son-in-law is as a yoke about the neck, since they must give him food and raiment and sustenance until he has learned to deal out his soup with his own ladle. And further—for must it not be said?—our daughter is not like other maidens, being stricken with a limp in her tongue, so that her words come haltingly and stumble one against the other. And these things need the sheen of money to cast a glamour over the eyes of suitors. For that she can repeat by heart three portions of Mishnah —what is it? It goes for nought in these ungodly days. And as for the tribulations that I have undergone or that are in store for me on this matter, I make light of them ; may they be taken for expiation of my transgressions and turn aside untoward punishment. Besides, is it not right and fitting that in all joyous occasion there should be some tinge of bitterness to make us mindful that we are exiles and abide in the midst of our adversaries?

First, then, I had recourse unto our townsmen that dwell in this city. And of them there is no inconsiderable number, nor indeed is there a region under the sun whereof one or two inhabitants are not congregated here—nay, not excepting Sheol and Tophet, for I have here seen stalking about devils blacker than ebony as to their skins and with many little horns of wool upon their heads ; but their tails were not visible, for the law of the land permits them not to go unclothed. But the townsmen, though they wished me well and received me hospitably, are poor men with scarcely a sufficiency of bread, nor do they live like God in Frenchland, as the saying is. So of them I could expect nothing. Then acting upon their advice, deeming it good, I went a different road. In this city there are men of our race whom God has blessed with riches passing the computation of man; they are said to eat from golden platters and to cast aside a garment after they have worn it but once. Now I thought it impossible that they would withhold from dispensing of their bounty unto me, a scholar and a poet from the crown of my head unto the toes of my feet. So then I sat me down, and with much labour and application I indited epistles unto them, setting forth their greatness and telling them of my urgent necessity. And the manner of my writing was such as no man on earth has attempted before. For in honour of the first man I composed an acrostic showing the initial letters of his name backward and forward, and with the end letters I dealt likewise. And the second epistle I wrote in the Aramaic tongue, with interspersions of Chaldee; and yet in a third I contrived that every seventh word should contain the sum total of the man's name reckoned by Gematrya. And various other and quaint devices of word-play I designed. And my reason for this was such—that these men, coming together at their banquets or in the House of Learning, and falling upon me for a topic, might say unto each other: "Clearly he springs not from the people of the soil, and his mind lingers not among the commonplaces of thought, but ranges boldly through the wildernesses and untrodden paths of conception; he is a man whom we must reward and honour for the honouring of ourselves and the congregation." And in this expectation I waited; and having waited for the space of a week I grew anxious and bewildered, for to all my missives there was no response. And I pondered many things, not knowing what to conjecture. Could it be that the messengers, whom they had entrusted with the bearing of their gift, had sequestered the money for their own use, defrauding me of my due and portion? But Leyb Tchariner inclined to this opinion: that my very wisdom had been my undoing, for that I had acted like a man who has dug a well of more than common depth for the obtaining of more copious water; but that the travellers from whom I expected reward for my toil, being men of despatch and haste, nor having sufficient length of chain to their own pitchers and disdaining to use another's, had hurried on without a second glance. And perhaps it was as he said; and as time went on and I heard nothing, I lost heart and set my thoughts in another direction, for I perceived that my affairs were going the crab's walk, that is, rearward and not forward.

And thereupon I bethought myself to set up a school for the teaching of our sacred tongue and for the instruction of youths in their portion of Holy Writ. But it proved a sore burden unto me, for the boys were unruly and troublesome, and neither were they attentive in their tasks nor in the payment of the lesson-money. And it chanced, unfortunately, that most of them were the children of Littvaks, and spoke a dialect unlike my own, which is Polish; and thus they said "Sibboleth," and what should be "hee" was "hoo" in their mouths. For this reason I was a mockery unto them, and one day they all by concert brought certain engines which they made to explode about my feet with sparks of fire and a loud reverberation. And upon that I fled from the chamber, nor have I returned amongst them to this day, for fear they might do me some bodily hurt. And in this extremity a plan entered into my head, hazardous in the accomplishing, but yet to be attempted. I have spoken before of Lutke, the same who turned informer; and it was in my heart to seek him, and reminding him of sundry benefits wherewith I had benefited him, and telling him that more blessed is he who gives than he who receives, to make appeal to him on my claim of clanship. But when I told my project unto the townsmen they laughed in derision: " What ails thee? Ask charity of Lutke? He will give—the calves which his oxen have borne him. Why, when we were building our synagogue and sent to him to make contribution towards the outlay, he said he would not deny us his help, but that he would give according to the deserts of the case. And on the following day there arrived a large casket, and our hearts were glad, for we thought: surely herein is some scroll of the Law, or some embroidered curtain to hang before the Ark ; but when we opened it, lo and behold, it contained three mouldy bricks and a block of worm-eaten wood—curses on the blasphemer! Rather husband thy dignity, and go not near him, lest he should make thee to wallow in the gutter of his abuse."

All this they said to me, but I did not heed them, being of advice that he would give ear to me though he had flouted the others; and besides, it benefits not a poor man to be dainty in his enterprises.

So then I took a little boy for my guide, having ascertained the man's abode. For who knew it not? Had they not all gone to look at the mansion wherein he dwelt, and to marvel why in this world the sinner is ever preferred to the righteous? And as for his wealth, they say it was acquired by the sale of cast-off clothing, and in other mysterious ways. Then having entrusted our bodies to the aforementioned contrivance that flies on the wings of fire and smoke, we were conveyed a long distance, and that—where shall the marvels cease?—below the level of the ground; and the texture of sulphurous gloom and horror through which it rushed was ripped into a thousand fluttering shreds. And only at given intervals did it rise to the surface, so that our vitals might not swell to bursting with the noisome vapours. But at last we alighted and came to Lutke's house, and I passed up the broad stairs of stone; and at my summons, straightway the doors were opened by two sons of Anak, white-haired and abruptly-clad as to their nether garments. And they stopped and accosted me. But their words were to me as the babblings of popinjays, and I heeded them not, crying with the full girth of my voice: "Lutke! Lutke!" And at the sound he came forth, the man himself—for I knew him at once by the indenting of the underlip where he had cleft it against the kerbstone in a drunken mood, and thou didst bandage it up with thine own hand. Then he looked at me, with an eye void of understanding, and said certain words to his hirelings. And then—as I live, I tell thee no falsehood—they gripped me by the shoulder, and jostled me, and thrusting me forth into the street, they shut the door with great violence. And so may the gate of Garden-Eden be closed in his face—I will not curse him overmuch, for are not all Israel brothers? Then it bitterly repented me of my foolhardiness, in that I had defied sager counsel. I had eaten to the full of vexation of soul, and my eyes were downcast with shame; for the little boy had witnessed all, standing by the outer gate, and he would spread the tale—are not children's mouths like sieves, through which their tongues trickle uncontainedly? But more than all, upon that journey I had expended one silver coin and two large pieces of copper, and my gain therefrom was not worth the tail of a rabid dog.

And on my return I kept steadfastly to my chamber, lest any one should feast his eyes on my humiliation. But on the third day a man, whose face I knew not, came to me and spoke many words and privily. And the import thereof was that for several years there had not appeared in this city a "Good Hebrew," and that the inhabitants, at least those that belonged to our faith, were swayed by many doubts and misgivings, and that there was much confusion in their households and private affairs, and there was no one to give them counsel or explain away their anxieties; that I, being versed in Kabbalistic lore and having penetrated deeply into the mysteries of heaven and earth, might fitly take such office upon me; and that there was much profit in the venture both for me and for him. Now the plan seemed good in my eyes, and we agreed. And he took upon himself the function of bedell and herald unto me, and caused it to go abroad that there had arrived a man of God, and all who were harassed by some trouble might come and he would salve them. And straightway our door became besieged by questioners. And Tyveles, the bedell, stood in the outer chamber and wrote the tablets and took the fee; and such as brought none or not sufficient he drove away, and would not let them enter the inner chamber where I sat and delivered responses. And those that came were chiefly women—maidens, past their first youth, who would know if they were ever fated to stand beneath the marriage canopy; mothers of ill-conditioned children, seeking a remedy for the curse; and lastly, matrons of long standing unto whom God had denied issue. To all these I replied according to the judgment which was in me. And this continued for several days; and in the night-time of each day

Tyveles would give me my share of the payments. But though I had suspicion that he gave not my due measure, I durst not say aught, for he was a man of fierce countenance and uncouth habits. At last, however, sinister rumours arose, and one day three men of accredited worth came and testified against Tyveles, how that he was an apostate, and had forsworn the faith, and had for long years consorted with the Gentiles; nor could Tyveles gainsay the accusers, for his falsehood lay manifest. So then the three men took hold of him and jostled him from the chamber with blows and other ill-natured treatment. As for me, I took upon myself a fast of three days to expiate the pollution of contact with the man. But mark how the evil ever beget evil. For certain calumniators rose up against me, saying that I had had foreknowledge of the man's misdoings and yet had taken him to my bosom and had broken bread with him. And the report gained credence, and thenceforth not a shadow darkened my threshold; even the townsmen looked askance and mistrusted me. Thus was I left to go my own way; and now the future lies dark before me, for

I know not unto which thing to betake myself. And my only hope is, by abiding here until the Great and Holy Days, which is yet two gatherings of the moon, to be chosen by one of the congregations to recite the Law and hold solemn discourse for the cleansing of their sins, for which they will make me remuneration and offer votive offerings on my behalf. And with this money I shall return to my country, and if it be not of the covenanted amount, verily our son-in-law that is to be must needs make an abatement thereon if he have set his heart upon our daughter in good sooth.

So then let this suffice thee for an account of me, and fear not, for the Lord forsakes not those who keep His ordinances. And these few precepts would I have thee lay to heart in the ordering of our household. As for the flesh which is my perquisite from the congregation, let it go towards the sustaining of thy life, so that neither thou nor our daughter may suffer hunger in the interval. But as for the suet that goes with the portion, let it be smelted and hawked about the town for sale, and all that accrues therefrom let it be laid by for the marriage. And if there be difficulty in the congealing of the fat, which might betide in this hot season, I would counsel thee to dig holes in the ground and therein to bestow it in covered pans; for it will meet with readier sale if it be hard and brittle. And the spot fittest for the bestowing methinks will be to the north side of our courtyard, where stands the great bay-tree that wards off the fierceness of the sun by its branches. And furthermore, in the feeding of our milch-goat, see that thou segregate the nightshade from the wholesome herbs, lest it die as happened with the other; and goatskin is a thing of small value, scarcely fetching the price of a fur collar against the winter. . . .

Glory be unto the Lord of Hosts! Knew I not that He would not withdraw His right hand from His beloved? This very instant there has been given to me thy second epistle which tells me glad tidings. A thousand roubles, sayest thou? Ay, ay! my heart leaps with joy, and my voice is raised in psalmody and thanksgiving. Surely it was God's own finger that turned the wheel of the lottery so that it stopped at the number of our billet. So then I shall despatch my affairs in this city, which are not considerable, and do thou prepare for my home-coming. For I shall follow close upon the heels and haunches of this missive.

THE MORDECAI OF THE SERFS

BY profession the two were "meshorrerim," which, of course, idiomatically rendered, means "journeymen synagogue minstrels"; but for everyday purposes of life we may call them choristers. Of the two, Klotz sang bass, and Avshalom tenor. Apart from this difference, they were great friends; their hearts beat in concord, and they swerved not from each other in truth or in falsehood.

For the benefit of those who might wish to adopt the calling, I shall here set forth in more detail the scope and function of such a "chorister." First of all you must possess a voice to sing with—a good one of necessity, an excellent one by preference. Then you must gain admission into the troupe of one of the "chazanim,"

THE MORDECAI OF THE SERFS

specifically "precentors," whose talents as such are too great to be supported by one single community, and who in consequence give devotional performances on tour. For instance, the proprietor of the choir to which Klotz and Avshalom belonged was Shaya Piper, whose headquarters were in Tamalov, which is in Lithuania, and whence he made choral incursions into the country around. If you are a little boy, you must take especial care lest you should be kidnapped by a rival itinerant company; such things are not unknown—therefore lay my words to your soul. You must furthermore be endowed with a versatile digestion; for each day you will be quartered on a different household for your dinner, and the fare ranges from roast goose to herring and potatoes—according to the means or the meanness of your hosts. If you have survived all this, you either become an operatic star in an American Reform Temple, or you marry the precentor's daughter and inherit the prestige and practice of your father-in-law.

At present, however, no such dreams of glory filled the bosoms of Klotz and Avshalom. Their hearts were heavy within them, despite the fact that this was the season of the "Feast of Lots," the joyous commemoration of Israel's escape from the spite of Amalek, when Haman and his sons were hanged on a tree ten cubits high—eleven according to some authorities; one might as well be impartial in these matters of history.

"Who among them did this deed of malice unto us?" asked Klotz, with reference to the cause of their affliction. The two had been walking cross-country for the last two hours, and by their rate of walking it seemed they had a whole purgatory of devils to walk out of themselves.

"I don't know," gasped Avshalom, on whom the exertion was beginning to tell, for he was not half as sturdy as his comrade—"no one in particular, unless it be Klumpka, the plate-licker; but they all hate us—thee, because thou art good to look upon and the maidens of the town make much of thee; and me, I know not, unless it be because thou hast taken me to thy bosom, after the manner of a brother, and so I share their hatred as I share thy love."

"The dogs!" growled Klotz. "All the

plagues of Pharaoh into their vitals. I never did one of them evil wittingly, for I am not a man who burns down his neighbour's house and steals his property in the confusion; but on me they had no mercy, and would grow rich in my despoiling. Let us go back, Avshalom—we cannot run away from our calamity, unless we walked all the way to Gehennom."

And upon their homeward journey their minds harked back for the twentieth time to the terrible scene of the morning, that had turned the Sabbath for them into a day of sorrowing. And this is what had happened. It was towards the end of the service; the synagogue was filled with the sound of praying-shawls being folded up and with the opening and shutting of seat-boxes, when a hush went through the assembly, for the preceptor of preceptors, the shining light of religion, even Rabbi Gamaliel himself, had risen from his seat and had stood before the Sacred Ark and had lifted up his voice:

"A woe and a sorrow which mine eyes have beholden will I relate unto you, my masters. It befell on the fifth day of the week, which was the Fast of Esther, that, upon a certain report which had reached me, I entered the dwelling-place of Shaya Piper, the precentor, at the hour when all his choristers were assembled, there to make inquiries into the state of their phylacteries and Four-corner garments. As to the Four-corner garments, I found that the rest were in fit condition, excepting that of Avshalom the tenor, whereof the fringes appending thereto were too short by half their ordained length, and that of Yashko Klotz the bass, which was none at all. And again what pertains to the phylacteries, all the rest were in fit condition excepting those of Avshalom the aforesaid, whereof one of the head-bands had been riven in twain, and those of Yashko Klotz, whereof the scroll of parchment had been removed from out of the leathern arm-capsule. And I bowed my head in affliction that this should be. But as to these two who have defiled the Name, I herewith decree, that during this Feast of Lots it shall not be lawful to ask them to join in the merrymaking, and that they shall go sequestered from all the congregation ; and furthermore, it shall be forbidden to them to make the quest with their pyxes for the messenger-gifts which it is customary to bestow upon this season. Thus have I pronounced in my wisdom and judgment, and unto this let us say Amen."

The Amen was scarcely appropriate, but as Rabbi Gamaliel had a habit of never saying two words without clinching them with an "Unto this let us say," the congregation duly responded "Amen"; and Klotz and Avshalom, from sheer stupefaction or from force of habit, joined in the response. But the others knew not from what cause they responded, and said that not only were they heretics, but also impudent faces.

Now, however, the full force of his disgrace came home to Klotz, and his bile seethed like a cauldron with the fire of his anger. That there had been a conspiracy he was sure. He knew that most of his fellow-choristers were but "righteousness clad in fur-skins," which translated means "wolves in sheep's clothing"; for none of them kept the appointed ordinances very strictly, and the fact that they had come without blot or blame from the ordeal of inspection was something more than accident. It was clear that some one had laid information against him and Avshalom and had warned all the others, so that they were prepared. And so this misfortune had come upon the two; and a misfortune it was, at least to Klotz—for the prohibition to quest meant a more serious loss to him than appeared on the surface. And now as he thought of the gibes and mocking looks from which he had fled and to which he was returning, he tore at his hair, beat his bosom, and said, "Woe, woe is unto me!"

"Let be," said Avshalom; "it is not good to afflict thy soul more than need be over this matter. The rascals — a black year upon them! But the time will come for our triumph. Be patient."

"It will come—but it must be soon," said Klotz, vehemently. "I had counted on the money," he went on more gently, "to send to my poor mother. She is a widow, and old, and she will be sorely in want, for I have sent her nothing ever since the Good Days; and then it was no great matter."

"I have two roubles and a half," suggested Avshalom.

"Which thou hast saved up in copecks to buy a pair of boots therewith," broke in Klotz. "No, little brother"—and he laid his hand caressingly on Avshalom's neck—"I will not take from my heart to give unto my soul. But let me consider—my head is choking with thought. I care not for other things—only I cannot think of her as starving," and his strong voice shook a little.

So they trudged on without another word till the chimneys of Tamalov hove in sight. Klotz came to a sudden standstill.

"Answer me, Avshalom," he replied; "whom of the villagers around dost thou take to be the most stupid and ignorant?—thou knowest the country."

"That is an easy question," replied Avshalom, readily—"those of Tarnagov, without a doubt. Why, they are more stupid than those of Chelm in Bohemia. Dost thou not know the tale how at a certain feast, whereat they all appeared in white trousers, they got so heavy with wine that they feared to rise from table lest each should walk away on his neighbour's legs?"

"I have heard the tale," said Klotz, "but I do not believe it—it is merely in a manner of speaking. Do they know Russian dost thou think?"

"Russian!" echoed Avshalom, disdainfully; "dost thou take them for scholars? They understand no language but their own; and we can talk that no worse than they — unless thou countest the grunting of their pigs and the bellowing of their bullocks at the plough for a language."

"King Solomon understood the language of many beasts—and he was a wise man," remarked Klotz.

"King Solomon understood because of his wisdom, and they understand because of their ignorance—that is the difference," answered Avshalom.

"Once more," said Klotz—"how far is it thither?"

"Two swift horses it will take less than three hours."

Avshalom wondered exceedingly at the drift of these questions; but Klotz did not choose to be explicit, and in that case it was no use pumping him.

"Let us walk more quickly," he said, resolutely; "and hold thy head high—let us not give the thieves cause to mock us by slinking along like whipped curs. And besides, I am hungry."

Avshalom said nothing, but wondered still more at the change of voice in Klotz and the look of determination—almost of exultation — that flashed from his eyes. What was in his mind?

The Sabbath was nearly over. On all sides the people were streaming to the House of Prayer, to hear the Book of Esther being read and to execrate Haman's memory and make sport of him in effigy. At the second corner they saw Shaya Piper and his choristers coming on in a body. Klotz did not swerve an inch, but linked his arm in Avshalom's and passed straight through their midst, nor did he turn his head at the gibes and laughter that broke from them in his rear.

"Let them laugh," he said, quietly; "I think I shall prick a big hole in their laughter and make it ring hollow."

Avshalom looked puzzled.

"Are we not going to the synagogue?" he asked.

"No," said Klotz, curtly—"they might ask us to sit on the mourners' seats; and besides, I have work to do that will be best done while we are alone."

Avshalom was a little afraid. He did not like missing the service, although the choristers did not assist thereat; but in the hands of Klotz he was as clay beneath the potter's thumb.

By now they had reached their place of abode. It consisted of three rooms, one of which was consecrated to Shaya and his wife—they had no children; the second served as a kitchen; and the third was a spacious hayloft, where the choristers slept on trusses of straw or anything that could be misconstrued into a bed.

"Let us get something to eat first—my stomach is whining piteously," said Klotz.

But the "getting something" was more easily said than done. Shaya's wife was economical—gossips called her miserly—and kept everything well under lock and key. But at last they found half a Sabbath loaf and five onions. Klotz devoured his share in silence, thinking busily all the time.

"Ah," he sighed, regretfully, after he had finished the last morsel, " glutton that I am, if I had not eaten so quickly, I should still be eating ; but blessed be God that there is no more, for a full stomach makes an idle brain. Let me get to my task, for clearly Providence is with me."

It was quite dark now, and three stars had come out to convoy the departing Sabbath ; but Klotz knew where the tallow stumps from the synagogue candelabra—one of Shaya's perquisites— were deposited. The way he set to work was peculiar. He went into the kitchen and there took a saucer of shoe-blacking, which, by the infusion of water, he converted into a make-belief for ink ; then he found a splinter of wood, which he sharpened into a stylus, and lastly helped himself to a huge sheet that served as fly-leaf to Shaya's Pentateuch. After that he sat down at the table and wrote. Avshalom looked over his shoulder in silent wonder ; Klotz was covering the paper with the letters of the Russian alphabet in every possible combination—for what purpose Heaven only knew, for Klotz was ignorant of the Russian tongue, and had never got further in the study of it than the shape of the letters. At last the two pages were filled, and weary work it had been, since it had worn away the stylus to half its original length and the patience of Klotz to its entire extent.

"There is just one thing more wanted," he said, looking with satisfied smile at his handiwork.

He took one of the lighted stumps, went up to the hay-loft, and in two minutes came down again, carrying in his hand a waxen seal large as a small plate.

"Where didst thou procure that?" queried Avshalom, in awe at his friend's resourcefulness.

"I tore it from Klumpka's slaughter-certificate; thou knowest he holds an authorisation to kill cattle—may he cut his own throat by mistake!" answered Klotz, unconcernedly; and with that he heated the wax and glued it firmly on to the paper in the empty space he had left in the right-hand corner at the top. Then he held the document at arm's length; it was indeed a stately and imposing affair.

"So far so good," he said, folding it up carefully and putting it in his pocket. "And now if thou art still willing to trust me with thy two roubles and a half till to-morrow—only till to-morrow," and he looked inquiringly at Avshalom.

The latter needed no further bidding, and Klotz took without a word of thanks the tanned goat-bladder that served alternately for purse and tobacco-pouch. These mutual accommodations were a matter of course.

"And now we must go to Chatzkel, the huckster, and see if we can find there what we want," said Klotz.

This particular Chatzkel—for his name is legion—kept a sort of co-operative store, and boasted that in his shop one could purchase everything—from tin-tacks to atoned transgressions, as he quaintly put it. Otherwise he was not a bad sort of fellow, and did many a little act of kindness in odd times and in odd places.

Klotz and Avshalom sallied out into the streets, and from every side there came upon their ears the sound of high revelry. Here and there they met with strange apparitions, boys and men in grotesque disguises—the masqueraders of the Jewish carnival. Avshalom's eyes followed them enviously into the houses, and he clenched his fist at the redoubled laughter that followed the maskers' entry. From all these joys he was an outcast. But Klotz made no sign at what he heard and saw. Chatzkel was behind his counter as they entered.

"I cannot give you anything; it is forbidden by the Rabbi's edict," he greeted them.

"I have not come for a gift, but for a loan," said Klotz, quietly.

"I only lend on deposit," returned Chatzkel.

"That, too, I have foreseen—here is money"; and Klotz displayed the vast amount of wealth which was his on trust.

"H'm, it depends; what do you require?" asked Chatzkel.

"If you have them," said Klotz, as if he were asking for an ounce of pepper, "I want a general's uniform, with cloak and medals; further, two false beards and a postilion's hat."

Chatzkel opened his eyes wide, and Avshalom nearly jumped out of his skin. He had thought they were going there to get a bottle of brandy and some honey-cake to make a little feast of their own. But all these absurdities—what were they for? Was Klotz mad?

"I know not what is the purpose of your disguise, nor how it will avail you," said Chatzkel, thoughtfully, after a while; "but if I have the things, you can take them and leave your money for a pledge."

So they followed him to his magazine, and he rummaged among the litter and the neatly-stacked bales, and behold!—did fortune favour them, or was Chatzkel really a great and wonderful man?—the articles were there. "What was there not?" as Chatzkel said, wiping his forehead, that shone with pride and perspiration. But he did not tell them why he was so good to them—that it was because he himself led a joyless, kinless life, and therefore could feel for them in their lonesome wretchedness.

"Stay with me this evening," he said, as he helped them making up their packages.

"I thank you, but I cannot; I am tired, my limbs feel all broken," replied Klotz—"and besides, it is not lawful."

"Ah, I forgot," said Chatzkel, with a sigh, as he watched them out into the darkness. But he kept the money. "They will be glad of it afterwards," he thought to himself. "Who knows? they might have gamed it away or spent it unworthily."

It was about ten o'clock when they reached home again. "We must get to bed straight away," said Klotz, "for we must be up early in the morning."

Avshalom was nothing loth; he was very tired—so tired, in fact, that he could not take the trouble to ask why Klotz fetched the stable-key that lay under Shaya's pillow and put it into his pocket; nor why Klotz placed the two straw-sacks on which they slept nearest to the door. Their bundles they had bestowed in the penthouse out in the courtyard, wherein Shaya's wife kept her geese for fattening from Tabernacles until the Festival of Lights.

The scent of the dawn was in the air when the others returned. They were none of them too steady about the legs, and as they stumbled up the staircase to the hayloft, guffawing and chattering, Klotz and Avshalom started up from their sleep.

"Look at them," jeered Klumpka, holding the candle over them, "where they lie in their beauty, David and Jonathan—they are dreaming of the riches they will gather to-morrow," and the others laughed. But the two gave no sign that they heard, and Klotz smacked his lips and threw back his head as was his habit to do during sleep.

And presently Klumpka got tired of his jeering and lay down. Klotz nudged Avshalom and whispered, "Keep awake, for as soon as they are asleep we shall go forth." And in another half an hour they got up quietly and stole down. They had to pass through Shaya's room; he heard them and sat up in bed.

"Who goes there?" he cried.

"It is I, Klotz—and Avshalom," was the answer in humble tones; "we are going to the Midrash-House, there to read in the Sacred Writ."

"There ye do well," yawned Shaya, "it will turn your minds to good, ye sinners in Israel, and may God pour grace and contrition into your hearts. No wonder evil dreams visit me at night; to think I have been sleeping all this time with two pair of desecrated phylacteries hanging over my bed "—for that was the regular place for the articles in question, so that they might serve as security against their owner's decampment.

Klotz quickly led the way to the penthouse, took up the bundles, and then passed on into the silent street down towards the shed that served for Shaya's stable; it stood half a mile beyond the town, but it was well protected, for the lock-chain was huge and massive, and the gates well fastened with clamps and rivets of iron. Avshalom followed drowsily, grumbling at his comrade's strange proceedings. Klotz quickly opened the gate and passed in.

"Don't stand there shivering, sleepyhead," he cried; "help me pull out the waggon and harness the horses—it will warm thee up."

In about ten minutes the conveyance stood ready. The waggon was large and roomy, the bottom littered with clean straw, with hurdles ribbing the length of both sides, and the two horses were strong and serviceable. Shaya used them to convey his company from place to place during his professional peregrinations.

Avshalom looked from the horses to Klotz and at last asked the question that had been trembling on his lips.

"Thou art not going to sell them?"

"No, simpleton, I am not a thief," came the indignant reply; "we shall bring them back before it is time to groom and fodder them; and now for our disguise."

It did not take him long to don his uniform; it was big enough to go over his own clothes, and made him look stalwart and broad-shouldered; and the cloak hid the folds that hung loosely in the back. Avshalom put on his postilion's hat and tucked his trousers into the shafts of his top-boots. And when they were ready Klotz jumped up and seized the reins, and away they went over the hard frozen ground; it was towards the end of February and the cold held the world with an iron grasp.

"Now wilt thou tell me what harebrained idea thou art harbouring?" asked Avshalom, getting seriously alarmed as to the outcome of their venture.

They had gone a good way already, and Klotz had talked about this and that and nothing at all.

"Willingly," he answered, "for we must concert our plans so that there may not be a hitch."

And then he told what it was in his heart to do; and as Avshalom listened his limbs began to shake, and he would have turned white if the cold had not already turned him blue.

"Thou madman," he said, through his chattering teeth; "we shall be discovered and they will tear us to pieces."

"Thou art very stupid," remarked Klotz, indifferently; "have we not been through worse things before?—hast thou forgotten how we escaped the recruiters at Ulsk?"

And then he gradually managed to talk a little courage into his faint-hearted ally; and what his persuasion failed to do was effected by a certain bottle of good size and better contents: Klotz had found it in the tail pocket of his uniform—for Chatzkel had thought that smuggling a gift did not come within the rabbinical edict. And so they went on, past the turf-stacks of Bavarak, past the flour-mills of Diabritz, past the cattle-pens of Vorshk. And between the admonitions of Klotz and the ministrations of the bottle, Avshalom beguiled the time in mumbling benedictory psalms on their enterprise. At last they caught sight of the birch-forest, the outposts of which skirted the houses of Tarnagov, their destination. Klotz now put the reins into Avshalom's hands and told him to drive at break-neck speed. So they rattled with tremendous clatter through the high-street, while every window flew open, and craning necks and gaping mouths protruded in multitudes. They pulled up at the tavern, and at the sound two ostlers rushed out. Avshalom jumped down and stood holding the horses' heads.

"Help his Excellency to alight," he whispered to the two men; "our state-carriage broke a wheel, and we had to come on in a ladder-cart. My master bears important despatches from St. Petersburg."

But Klotz grandiosely waved aside their assistance, as though he did not like them to lay hands on him, and got out with much ceremony and circumstance.

"What, is there no one here to receive a messenger of the Government?" he roared, pulling himself up to his full height, which exceeded that of an ordinary man. And without further ado he strode towards the house, closely followed by Avshalom.

On the threshold they were met by the host, hot and breathless. " Pardon your honour," he said, " I was kennelling my bloodhounds—they are very fierce to-day, and the horses——"

Klotz stopped him with a wave of the hand. " I cannot have long speeches, for I am in haste," he said ; "let the town-crier go out and bid all the heads of families assemble here within the hour, and let those that cannot come send their proxies. I bear an imperial rescript."

"Your will shall be done," said the host, bowing low, for he was struck with awe at the stranger's voice and demeanour.

Klotz sat down by the chimney fire in solitary grandeur, while Avshalom stood whispering with the host, and told him what Klotz had enjoined him to say. And sure enough, in a little time the tavern began to fill with peasants—for this was Sunday, and Klotz had taken that into account; and they all stood in the furthest corner casting anxious, sidelong glances at him, while Avshalom went amongst them and spread the tale of his master's greatness. More and more peasants came, and a hum of eager excitement surged through the crowd. What was going to happen? What were they going to hear? Was there some new oppression, some new disability to be laid on them in addition to those beneath which the poor serfs already groaned? And each man looked anxiously at his neighbour.

At last the host came forward on tiptoe and whispered, "My lord, we are assembled."

Then Klotz got up leisurely, threw back his cloak, so that all could see the glitter of his sham stars and crosses, and stood eyeing them disdainfully; slowly and deliberately he unfolded his document, lifted his cap, and reverently kissed the great seal.

"In the name of the Czar," he began, and that glorious deep voice of his seemed to travel into the caverns of the earth, and thence to reverberate with redoubled volumes of sound; and a tremor quivered through the assembly. "Whereas we have decreed, in our great mercy and in our all-pitiful goodness of heart to seek the welfare of the peoples under our dominion : it shall be established henceforth as a law and a statue unto all ages that servitude shall cease amongst our subjects, and that every man shall be master of his body and his chattels and all that appertaineth unto him ; and that it shall not be lawful for any Lord of Manor to claim tithe and tribute of him, and the strength of his sinews shall no more be expended in tilling the feudal lands, but he shall be permitted to husband his own, and to reap the labour of his hands in his own garner and his own threshingfloor. And this shall obtain throughout the length and breadth of our rule. And herewith we send messengers to proclaim the good tidings unto all such whom it shall benefit even in the tongue that is severally understanded of them ; and we have set upon it the warranty of our Great Seal. Furthermore we make known that whosoever shall suffer violence or encroachment upon these rights, unto him it shall be given to vindicate them with might and main, even to the wielding of arms. And in token of this we authorise our messengers to enact a liberation-tax of one-half silver rouble per head of family to augment the exchequer of the empire. Long live the Czar."

Such was the term of the proclamation; and for some time after the reading the heavy hand of surprise lay on the mouths of the listeners and kept them mute; then there came little ebullitions of sound that were like the wind that rasps through the trees and tells that the thunder is coming. But it did not suit Klotz that their feelings should find vent; it was best that their thoughts should remain cumbered down by their unuttered amazement. So in business-like tone he continued:

"Silence all: quick, host, get me pen and paper—for my portfolio was left in my carriage—so that I may write down the names of all who seek enfranchisement; for these are to be registered in the archives of the land to be a charter to them and their children and their progeny afterwards; and forget not the tax."

Then there began a crush and commotion to get to the table where Klotz was seated, each one striving to be the first enrolled on the list of the emancipated; and those who had no money on the spot either borrowed it from their friends or loaned it from the tavern-keeper on security of rings and snuff-boxes and suchlike. For it had come at last, the blessed hour of freedom for which they had pined and whined; now they would know what life meant; now they could drink one half the time and idle half the other, whilst their wives saw to the potato crop and tended the pigs—it was glorious. And the tax—it was that which proved the genuineness of the rescript. Was there ever a rescript issued for good or ill whereto there did not hang an impost? So Klotz wrote down the name and trade of each man in his turn, and Avshalom raked in the money; his fingers trembled a little—no doubt on account of the cold. At last it was all over, and Klotz got up, stretched himself mightily, and said, " Brothers—for we are that now, brothers and peers—I must hasten on to carry the good news further; and when my carriage comes here tell my servants to seek me on the road to Minsk. Let us go," turning to Avshalom; " health and great riches upon you all."

With that they passed out, and everybody stood out of their way with deep obeisances, and one or two made even bold enough to print a kiss on the corner of the mock-messenger's cloak.

"Drive hard, for the love of Heaven," whispered Klotz; for now that his object was accomplished he felt his heart falling between his feet, and his blood was congealed into clots with fear. But as he put his foot on the axle a loud shout was heard and a man came running towards them frantically. Klotz and Avshalom turned pale and looked at each other.

"For mercy's sake," panted the man, when he came near, "do not go before you have added my name. I was belated, and my brother came to seek me lest I and my household should remain in servitude when all the others went free."

Klotz waited a moment, till his own breath went steady again. "What is thy name?" he asked, severely.

"Ivanov Shleutra, and I am the carrion-carter of this place, your honour."

"Ivanov," continued Klotz, "thou shalt go free like the rest, but for thy remissness the penalty shall be one whole rouble over and above the half."

And that was a rouble on which they

had not reckoned; but they thought that it was more hardly earned than all the rest put together. And the whole amount, as they counted it, came to seventy-three roubles and a half, not to mention the four coins that were spurious. But they did not laugh till they were again well on the road to Tamalov; they had doffed their disguises long ago, and when finally they had restored the horses and vehicle to their proper abode, then only was it that they felt the rock of anxiety lifted from off their bosoms.

They had met nobody, for it was the hour of the midday meal, and no one stirred abroad lest he should be cheated out of his portion of the three-cornered meat-dumplings that were the speciality of the day. So they walked on to Shaya's house, while Avshalom now and then peeped sideways at his companion, like a mortal who had long sojourned with a god and knew it not.

When they came in, dinner was finished, and all the choristers were there—for Shaya had behaved handsomely and had feasted them at home that day; and now they sat, each for himself, taking stock of the money which that morning's questing had brought him. The harvest had been but scanty. Some had taken no more than two roubles; but Klumpka had managed to obtain three roubles twenty copecks and a big bruise on the right side of his forehead. How he came by that was not known; later on it was current that he had climbed to the garret of a poor bedridden cripple, whence he would not depart till the indignant neighbours pitched him downstairs. Klumpka denied the report—but then, why was he called the "plate-licker"?

"Here come the Korahs, the wealthy men," he jeered, as he caught sight of Klotz and Avshalom; "where have ye quested? In the House of Everlasting Life—among the tombstones?"

"Yes," said Klotz, "the dead are generous—they have given me richly; listen," and he jingled the silver in his pocket. "Why, I can even afford to give thee five copecks to buy a plaster for thy bruise," and he threw the coin at his feet.

"Thou hast stolen it," screamed Klumpka.

"Then wait till the robbed comes and

makes complaint," answered Klotz, and busied himself among the scraps and bones that remained from the meal; he was content, for he knew that his mother would have better fare for many a day to come.

Now in this adventure of Klotz there were several things that gave cause for wonder. First of all the choristers wondered what danger it was that Avshalom had escaped so that he offered public thanksgiving for his deliverance and paid a rouble in token of his sincerity; and further, where he had obtained the rouble. Then Abihu, Shaya's groom, wondered why, when he came to tend the horses, he found them so broken-winded. Furthermore, Klumpka wondered who it was that had torn the seal from his slaughter-certificate. Again, the whole province wondered what spirit of madness had come over the peaceful peasantry of Tarnagov, that they should refuse their serf-labour when called upon to do so by the overseers and taskmasters, so that the police had to come with staves and blunt bayonets to force them to their toil and stop them babbling about rescripts and emissaries and liberty charters. And finally Klotz and Avshalom wondered what manner of Providence it could be that turned the evil which man designed against man into a source of blessing and augmentation.

"WHOSE JUDGMENT IS JUSTICE"

> While the heavens stand firm, to the world's last term
>   Shall be the three things that were from the start:
> The word of God—His chastening rod,
>   And the suffering-strength of a woman's heart.
> *Saying of the Fathers* (interpolated).

"AND thou weepest because thou hast lost a child that was not even yet a weanling? And therefore thou walkest here in solitude by the edge of the lake, wringing thy hands and crying aloud in the bitterness of thy heart? Ah, blessed are the young in their strength! Seest thou not how thou art blessed in being strong to wash the sorrow from thy soul through the floodgates of the eyes? But in us that are old the sluices are weary with flowing, and therefore the grief remains unmoved, and lies heavy as a stone; and by reason of its endurance it becomes as part and parcel of our lives, so that we would not grow rid of it, even if we could. Therefore I begrudge thee not thy tears; but lest thou shouldst arraign Heaven and thereby bring sin upon thy head, I would have thee remember that whomsoever God loves He chastises. And me He has loved very much. Have I not lived to the age of sixty—and I know not how much over—and have I not been stricken very hard? One child thou didst lose, and one that had not learned to bite with its teeth? But I have lost four that were long past the pitfalls of infancy, and were like to grow up as cedars of Lebanon. But the great woodcutter, which is the Angel of Death, cut them down—two of them singly and two of them at one stroke; for at that time he was in great haste, and worked busily with his hands. So while we sit here in the cool of the evening, let me tell thee the tale of my four children; but do thou, my daughter, on no account remit thy weeping.

"One son I had, and his name was Isaac—what am I saying?—nay, it was Benjamin, of whom I must tell thee first.

He had grown to be thirteen, and already I was casting about my eyes among the maidens of the place to choose him a wife. Verily, he was a lad who might be a joy to his mother, and right willingly did he take upon himself the burdens of the household; for his father had gone betimes to prepare places for us all in Paradise. And this was the period of the Cantonists. What, thou knowest not of the Cantonists? Ah, I forgot that thou comest from afar, even from across the frontier, and the tale of them has not reached thy ears. Nor indeed is it fit for the ears of women, for it is a tale of darkness and misery and the rending of hearts. But for the purpose in hand it must needs be told thee at length and with a full mouth.

"It was in the time when Nicolai ruled over the land, and his councillors put an evil thought into his mind, like the thought of Pharaoh when he set his heart on the harassing of the children of Israel. And was there not sufficient of tribulation before? God knows all things, and whom He loves He chastises. And this, then, was the evil in the matter of the Cantonists. For the heads of the

"WHOSE JUDGMENT IS JUSTICE" 245

provinces and the governors of the towns and the mayors of the villages looked with jealous eyes on our people, how their offspring waxed great by the blessing of God unto Abraham. And therefore they said craftily to one another:

"'Let us lay hands on the little children which are the roots of a nation growing into and strengthening the bulk of the trunk.'

"And then there was issued an edict which provided that youngsters ranging from the age of eight to fifteen, which is implied in the meaning of the word—since thou knowest not the language—should be taken from the homesteads of their birth and scattered about the country.

"Now this was the method of the taking. Over each village there was set a warden, and chiefly he was a man of our own faith, for he had most cognizance of the families of his brethren. And from this warden it was required that when called upon he should furnish boys from the children of the congregation to the number that was named. At first the people understood not this plague that had come upon them; but when presently one child was kidnapped and then another, and the calamity spread abroad, then indeed there rose a wail of sorrow that might have shook the gates of heaven. But the heavens are planted upon firm foundation, and therefore they did not fall and crush the heads of the evildoers. And mostly there suffered the poverty-stricken, for they could give no gifts to make propitious to them the hearts of those that held this matter in hand; and so when a rich man's son was named for a victim, his father would go and prevail by bribery, so that there was a substitute. And surely there must be some great dispensing of God's favour upon this generation, that their eyes behold not what ours saw in those days. For our village lay full in the route of the children's journey; and they came in bodies of hundred, with the riders at their side and in their back—and the riders bore kantchouks in their hands that lay not idle. And through each rank there ran a leathern thong for a tether, fastened to the sleeve of each, lest at dark of night any should escape. For they marched day and night, huddled in their long mantles of raw hide that trailed over their feet and made them to stumble; and whenever they slept it was by the roadside or in the ditches, so that their garments were caked with muddy slime, unless the season was frosty and the ground stiff and unyielding. But from every hundred that went forth barely two or three returned; and that was because their hands and feet were bitten useless with the cold and their hearing was numbed so that they heard not. As for the rest, this was the fate that befell them. They were penned up like cattle in stables until creeping sores and diseases fastened upon them from want of food and storing room. Now those for whom there was hope of recovery, they were given to the peasants for the tending of their swine, and the yoke was laid upon them to draw furrows like oxen; and twelve of them went to one ox. But as for those that were rotten to the core and in whom the cancers had eaten the flesh to the bone, for these were built large wooden sheds, and an opiate was mixed in their food. And at night, when they slept, there were lighted great trusses of wet straw, whereof the fumes penetrated the chinks, and during their sleep was their innocent life choked out of them.—What, thou dost not believe? See, I am near to the end of my days, and what would I gain by accusing my fellow-creatures idly? But these things happened as I have said, nor did I see a windmill where there was but a cow; rather have I been niggardly in my setting forth, for there are many to whom the memory of this still comes as a nightmare in the broad of the day. And each time when a troop had passed through, the parents would look at each other with leaden eyes, and turn their faces from their children; but in those days many a beard of brown whitened into snow overnight. Such, then, is the story of the Cantonists, and I had a son Benjamin.

" Now thus far I had escaped the visitation. And I knew not to what to ascribe my good fortune, unless it was because of my sister, who had now been a faithful servant for twelve years at the house of the Davoustchik, which is the Warden. And seemingly at her entreaty, my son Benjamin had remained exempt. But the time came when for the great part the available youngsters had been despatched, and there were left behind only the children of the wealthy, and the children of the Warden and of his kinsfolk, and the child that was mine, even my son Benjamin.

"And one night my sister came bringing me word that there was at last no thrusting off the impending doom, for that the kidnappers were ordered to seize my son Benjamin on the morrow. Yet though the dismay was great in my heart, I did not fold my arms idly, making no attempt to wrestle with fate. For of furtively slipping away there was no question, since the issues of the place were watched; but in my head there had been ripening a plan against the emergency. Therefore at dead of night I awoke my son—for he slept soundly in ignorance of the danger—and told him what there was to be done. And the boy looked up at me wildly and said:

"'Mother dear, I am afraid.'

"And then I urged him again, saying that there was no other outlet from the disaster, and that all must be staked on this throw. Thus we sat during the night, and his arms clung about my neck and there was a trembling through all his body.

But towards the morning he grew calmer and at last he said:

"'Mother dear, if this must be done, then I shall not resist, for I cannot bear to see thy grief; but I am afraid—afraid unto death.'

"And then in all haste I took a linen sheet from my couch, and placed two chairs for a trestle, and laying my son Benjamin thereon, I covered him with the sheet; and further, I lit two candles and set them on the floor near his head. So then we waited; and after some time of waiting I heard the kidnappers outside, and rushing to the door I flung it open with a loud cry.

"'You have come too late—my son Benjamin died at the rising of the sun; look where I have laid him out for burial.'

"And one of the men—there were two—said according to the formula, 'Blessed is He whose judgment is justice.' And then he shouldered past me, for I dared not prevent him, and strode up to the chairs and lifted a corner of the sheet; and turning to the other he said, 'She speaks truth; we have come too late—he is dead.'

"Then he passed out, and on the threshold I caught his hand and quickly pressed therein a silver coin, for that he had borne me out and had saved my son Benjamin. And the man looked at me with big eyes and said nothing. And then I watched them passing down the street, giving praise to God for my deliverance, and thinking quickly that I should have an empty coffin taken from my house, and conceal my son Benjamin in his chamber till I might smuggle him away into safety. And at last, when the men were out of sight, I flew to the boy, and snatched off the covering and called him; but he slept on, worn out with the watching of the night. And then I shook him, and kissed him on the mouth—and at that his jaw fell, and I saw what I saw. And the coffin that went from my house was not empty. Aye, blessed be He whose judgment is justice. But what is this? I charged thee to weep, and yet thy tears come less plentiful for thy child that was not even a weanling.

"And now let me tell thee of my daughter Esther, that went by the name of Hadassah, the myrtle, because her breath was as a fragrance and the bloom lay on her face summer and winter; and her full tale of these was fifteen. And to all her lovers who asked her in marriage she gave one answer: 'I shall not go from under my mother's roof; for since my brother Benjamin died there is no one to bring grist to the mill, so that she and the two little ones'—meaning the two youngest, that were twin—'may not go hungering.'

"Now the manner of our occupation was the growing of herbs and vegetables, which she went to sell in the houses of the town. But there was none that paid with more liberal hand than the Galach, I say the village priest, an old man and pious and walking in the fear of God. And about this time he died, and there was put in his place a young man, a wolf in sheep's clothing, who wrought evil things in secrecy. And the third time my daughter went to his house she returned with flaming cheeks:

"'Mother, the Galach has reminded me that I am a woman grown.' And thereafter it was I who carried him the produce of our field. And often he made inquiry after my daughter with feigned kindliness, though I knew it was with no good purpose; nor was there once that he passed my house without spying into the doorway. And one day he entered, asking me, 'Have you perchance seen a spaniel of mine that has gone astray?' And just then my daughter came in, and he said further:

"'Behold, I went out to seek a hound, and instead I have found a Rose of Sharon.'

And thereon she answered rashly and without wisdom:

"'The thing that you find had liefer be a hound than a Rose of Sharon.'

"And he bit his lip, and, looking her full in the face, he said, 'So even the Roses of Sharon have thorns that sting? Yet none the less are they desirable for culling.' And so he continued harping on the word in terms of insult.

"And that was not the only time, for after that he came often to the house, and I had not the courage to gainsay him entrance; and further, I besought Esther, if she could not hie from the chamber in time, to show him courtesy and meet cunning with cunning. But what could two women avail against him who wrought by the aid of Satan? And when my daughter disappeared, just as a stone is dropped into a well, even then he came and asked for her presence; and when I told him she was not, he laughed at me in my distraction, and said:

"'You have hidden her for fear of me, and that is unkind of you, for I am a man of God and would do wrong unto no living thing.'

"And he said it so speciously that for long time I was swayed by doubt whether his ignorance was feigned or true, in the meantime making diligent inquiry in the neighbourhood, and enjoining the fishers to give heed when they dragged the river for fish. And the time passed on without tidings.

"But after some weeks the priest came to me saying, 'You did right to bewail your daughter. I have this day come from Warsaw, and there I have seen the Rose of Sharon trailing in the mud of the gutters, beneath the light of the lanterns; and her name is a byword in every tavern for ten miles around.'

"And from that I knew that he lied, for at Warsaw, in the old cemetery, her father lies buried, and she would not dare to do evil in a place where his soul could lay its finger on her as she passed. And, moreover, I knew now that the priest had a hand in her vanishing.

"So I bided my time, and one day, having watched him depart on his conveyance, I went to his house, there to converse with the old woman who tended his kitchen, and I took with me a slice of honey-cake and a bottle of raisin wine in strong fermentation.

"'There, Katrinka,' I said, 'I have brought thee a gift that will please thee—the cake is soft and needs no teeth-grinding, and the wine will run like fire through thy body.' So then we sat talking, and I plied her cautiously with questions; and at last the wine loosed her tongue, and she spoke. 'Aye, aye,' she said, 'it is a dreary life and solitary I lead here since the old priest died, for my new master has much business abroad and is no stay-at-home; but latterly he goes often to the convent of Tchenstochov, doing good service to a novice, and curing her of the devil that is strong within her.'

"And then I knew where I had to seek

for my daughter; and having awaited the priest's return, and also having bestowed my two other children with an affinity of mine, I set out for the convent, two days' journey on foot, for perchance God would show me a way to wrest her from her adversaries. And on the way I stained my teeth with saffron and my hands and face with walnut, so that I might go unknown; and further, that I might have a pretext for not knowing their language, feigning to be a gipsy.

"Now when I had arrived, which was in the morning of the third day, I straightway hid among the bushes that hedged the courtyard of the convent. And not long after there came out two she-priests, leading between them a third that wore a thick veil of black about her head so as to shut off all her sight. And as they led her up and down, I knew her for my daughter Esther by the upward jerk of her arms which had been her habit as a child, and much I marvelled that the habit should have come back to her after such long time. But I took the encounter for an omen and a sign that she would soon be released from her captors. So each day I watched, but except for a sight of my child I gained nothing.

"At last came a time when she no longer appeared, and I waited in vain for her coming. But a week later, as I stood clawing at the fence in my distress so that the blood sprang from the nails, a man came out on the terrace and stood looking about. And at last his eyes chanced on me, and he cried: -

"'What dost thou there, thou vagabond? Come in and earn a meal honestly if thou wouldst, so that thou hast no need of pilfering.'

"And at the bidding I tremblingly passed in through the gate, not knowing what this might betide. And then it appeared that one of the charwomen had fallen in a faint, and that I was to do her portion of the work. And from the talk of the others I learned that on the morrow there was to be a great solemnity, because of the dedication of a novice. And then I knew that the knife was at my throat and that there was great need of a miracle.

"Now it chanced that I was stationed upon the second floor, and on my right hand there was a door whence I heard voices—one voice that spoke with a loud eagerness, and a second whose words came faint and languid. And as I lay there on my hands and knees listening with all the might of my ears, the door was opened and out came the selfsame priest I knew, red and angry, and in passing he darted at me with his foot, bidding me move out of his way. And when he was gone I gently lifted up the latch and peered into the chamber; and there, stretched out all her length on the couch, lay my daughter Esther, or, at least, the shadow of her. And at sight of me she gasped, 'Mother, mother, come quickly—they have killed me!' for she knew me despite my disguise, and from that I augured that she was dying, for the dead know all things. And I flew to the couch, and cradling her head on my bosom, I bade her repeat the attestation of Israel: 'Hear, the Lord is thy God!' And her lips moved faintly in struggling after the sound, but her hands kept ever jerking to her neck as I had seen her do in the courtyard, but she had not strength to lift them high enough. And at last I understood, and, unfolding her dress, I saw upon her heart a crucifix of jasper; and snatching it up, I flung it upon the ground, so that it shivered into a thousand pieces. And at that she raised her head and said, 'Thanks, mother dear; I could not die with that on my——' And she breathed once more, and only once more. Then I kissed her and said, 'Blessed is He whose judgment is justice,' for that they had only killed her body, but not her soul.

"And at that moment there came in three of the she-priests, and they stood looking at me and my daughter and the fragments on the floor. But I had my tale ready: 'I heard a loud cry, and entering here, I found the maiden dying; and just before she died the Mother of God there'—and I pointed to the large image in clay that was placed on a shelf over the couch—'stretched out her hand, took the crucifix from the maiden's bosom, and hurled it upon the floor. And all this I saw with my own eyes, and can testify to the miracle.'

"And they dared not deny my word, for that would be casting a doubt on the Mother of their God. And after I had got me forth from the convent I rent my garment, and waited till the following day to see them bury my daughter; and in the night I came and tore down the cross that had been fixed over her grave, and planted around the place a circle of pebbles, so that she might lie apart from the Gentiles. After that I hurried away to my native place, there to sit through the ordained period of mourning.

"Thus did I lose my daughter—aye, blessed be He whose judgment is justice! But wherefore hast thou ceased weeping, thou that didst just now make such lamentation for thy child that had not outgrown its swathing-clothes?

"And now there remained to me but two—Isaac and David, that were born at one birth. And when I looked at them I knew that my old age would not go tottering along without two strong staves to lean upon. But alas! it was my doom to be a childless mother of children, and had I borne a hundred I should only have been childless a hundredfold—but blessed be He whose judgment is justice! And the two were taken off in a manner that has no like within the memory of men—even by the hand of one another were they taken off and died.

"Truly thou art a stranger in this land, yet hast thou heard of the great uprising wherewith the people of this country were uplifted against their oppressors, for the fame thereof has flooded the world even as their blood flooded the soil of their fathers. But nowhere was the earth redder than there where flowed the blood of my twin sons, Isaac and David. For they heeded not the voice of their mother, but said, 'Counsel us not to our shame so that it be said, "Oh, this valiant progeny of the Maccabees!—look how these cocks crow each on his own dunghill!" For we are mindful of our brother Benjamin, that died by the tyrant, and we have not forgotten our sister Esther, that died through the curse of his superstition; and for every hair of their head we shall slay one of his servants.' Thus they spoke, talking big words as is the wont of boys. And Isaac had lately married, and he said to his wife, 'Fear not; I shall return by the time I can look at the face of my child.'

"So they went forth with the rest, and fought the battles of their countrymen.

And we women sat at home and fought against their evil destiny with prayers and supplications; and our fighting, too, was not without its bloodshed. And suddenly we heard of the great battle that had been fought at Bialablotta, the place of the chalk mud, and that the Emperor's men had prevailed and had driven their enemies—the brothers-in-arms of my sons—before them, and had slain them in multitudes. And a great band of the fugitives had fled within two miles of our village and were encamped in the forest, where they would lie in wait for their pursuers.

"And the whole tenor of the calamity was related to us by one of the fugitives that escaped the slaughter; and I remember his words distinctly, for I drank them in, not with my ears, but with all the soul that is within me. And this is what he said: 'It was in the gathering of the darkness that we heard the trampling of hoofs from afar, and from the sound we knew that the Cossacks were coming. So we got ready, standing behind the trees on either side of the road, intending to close in upon them as they passed through and make havoc of them in our midst. But the Cossack is a child of the devil by a she-fox; and thus it was that they escaped destruction by the pricking of a horse-ear. For the stallions on which they rode became restive, tossing their heads and sniffing the air; and from that their riders knew that there were mares ahead—likely the mares of some transport. But as none of their comrades had passed in front, they guessed that some body of the enemy lay across their road. So, laughing at their own shrewdness, they dismounted, and waited till the dark had come on full. And then they picked out a hundred of their horses that were of least store, tied upon their backs a corpse, wherever they could find one—and the search was easy—and sent them galloping upon our trail. And we, hearing them advance, stood waiting with our weapons in our hands till the squadron had come up; and then we rushed forth and started hacking at them with our knives, for we dared not shoot for fear of assistance coming to them. And how it was we knew not. There was no moon, and the trees towered high like great fingers pointing to heaven in accusing of the horror; but, meeting no resistance, we fought and hacked and slaughtered, until suddenly we found other weapons darting at our bosoms, and we thought that the enemy had worked up his mettle. Then we returned the stabs with twofold vigour, and not a cry was uttered even by those in their death agony, for that was against the command. And we thought that now we were avenged; but just then came the first streak of dawn, and we saw what we had done, and how our madness had betrayed us into self-destruction. And there lay four hundred of us whom our own arms had sent into the last great sleep.'

"Thus much he told us, and the rest I learned for myself. For early in the morning, when we heard of the carnage, we went forth with fomentations and bandages to help the wounded, for we thought, 'Thus may other mothers go forth to ease our sons when they suffer.' And I was the foremost, and went amongst the bodies, turning them over and feeling their hearts; but most of them were still, for whose hand strikes more surely than that of a friend or familiar?

"And at last I came to where lay two bodies close to each other, with their left hands clasped tightly and their lips almost touching; and the dagger of the one stuck in the throat of the other, and the knife of the second gashed the bosom of the first. And at the sight a faintness came over me, and I crept up to them on my knees, averting my head with dire forebodings; and when I turned it—it was like twisting it from the foundations of my neck—and looked, why, behold— blessed be He whose judgment is justice! —there were my two sons Isaac and David, or they that had been my sons, for now they belonged to the earth whereof their bodies were made. And with the strength of three I dragged them among the trees and covered them with my headcloth; and then I ran to fetch Naomi, Isaac's wife, who was a mother of eleven days, and said to her, 'Quick! bring thy babe, so that it may look once upon the face of its father, for he will never look upon the face of his child— blessed be He whose judgment is justice!'

"And I took with me a hand-waggon, and laid thereon my two sons, and conveyed them to the 'Good Place,' lest they should be deposited with the others in the great hole that served for the common sepulchre.

"These things have I seen and done, and I have eaten to the full of child-sorrow, and they were none of them sucklings like thine. What is this? Dry-eyed? Truly it is said that a small grief melts away in the telling of a greater. And now let us go, since the night air is chill, and here comes my grandson searching for me; for the love he bears me is as great as half the love I have buried in the graves of my four children."

COSSACK AND CHORISTER.

ANYBODY with half an eye to proportion could see what an ill-assorted couple they were. Among their most obtrusive dissimilarities were these : the one was called Casimir, the other Jacob—the names betokening Slav and Semitic descent respectively. Again, Casimir had to stoop under most of the doorways through which he passed, whereas Jacob, when standing his tallest, just reached Casimir's elbow, a circumstance to be explained by the fact that the one had been a full-grown man for years, while the other had still most of his growing to get through. But the most radical difference surely was this : Casimir was a spear-bearing, fierce-whiskered member of his Majesty's imperial army—Cossack department; and Jacob a soprano chorister in the local synagogue. How, in spite of these desperate inequalities, there came to be any connection between the two was a miracle.

It is the fashion to explain miracles by natural causes; this was a case in point. To bring about primarily a reachable distance between Casimir and Jacob, it was fated that certain turbulent minds among the gentry of the district wherein Jacob lived should become suddenly troubled by the ghosts of Sobietski and Kosciusko and the spectre of Poland's departed greatness that came to them clamouring for a speedy re-incarnation. These turbulent minds had long failed to see what connection—excepting that of the railway—there should be between St. Petersburg and Warsaw, and why people should not be allowed to do as they liked in and with their own country. They thereupon took to disseminating this opinion, at first privately and with circumspection, then more broadcast and openly, until rumours of it reached the keenset ears of the governmental authorities, who with great gusto straightway made a blood-curdling report of it to headquarters. There is a fixed and constitutional remedy for these cases of political hay-fever, administered in the shape of two or three Pulks of Cossacks, whose presence generally serves as a cooling-draught for the hot-headed restorationists. That is how Casimir came to Lotz.

There was a great deal of excitement when the regiment rattled into the little town and halted on the market-place. Everybody was there to receive them—from the mayor to the knacker, just to show there was no ill-feeling towards the arrivals, and the patriots felt very small at sight of the swarthy bearded faces and gleaming lance-points. Of course Jacob was there, bearing himself very calmly in the possession of a clean conscience; but all the same, he felt rather frightened when presently one of the men rode straight up to him and said, gruffly:

" Do you know one Pototski, a miller?"

There was nothing formidable about the question, and Jacob felt particularly adapted for answering it.

" Yes, I know him," he piped; " my mother lives in his courtyard."

" Come along, then, and show the way—I am billeted there," said the man; and before Jacob knew what was happening he found himself whipped up by the nape of his jacket and seated astride in the saddle. In a second or two he grew alive to the situation, and determined to make the best of it. Horse-riding was a new sensation to him; when his father, who had been a butcher, was living, he had occasionally been allowed to ride cattle to the shambles. But this was different; to ride on one horse with a Cossack was an experience to relate and remember, and would no doubt raise his prestige among the knickerbocker population of the town by several inches.

This was the first contact between Casimir and Jacob, but it needed more than that to bring about an acquaintance. And this time, despite the shoulder-shrug of the rationalist, the hand of Providence was stretched forth visibly. Two days after, Jacob was sitting near the window to catch the last streaks of the dying daylight; for he was particularly anxious to finish carving his bulrush whistle that evening. It was turning out beautifully— the rind was tough and fresh, and would not require much hammering to remove the stalk from within, and Jacob expressed his satisfaction thereat in tones of loud and clear-voiced melody. He did not notice what he was singing—singing had become a mechanical action with him; he sang with as little self-consciousness as a bird, and therefore, because his music came from the heart, it went to the heart. In the distance there was a sound of rioting, where the soldiers had gathered in the canteen; but sometimes, when Jacob's voice rose especially clear, there was a lull as if they were listening. Jacob noticed neither the noise nor the silence, but worked on busily. His mother sat at the table with a pile of goose-feathers before her; she was stripping the down from the quills to make feather coverlets of them—it was what she earned her living by.

The twilight waned, and the room was filled with the argent glimmer of the full moon. "We shall save a rushlight to-night—God is good," thought Jacob, and sang on. Just then there was a sound of heavy steps walking as though trying to tread down their heaviness; they came nearer, and paused before the door. Jacob heard them, and stopped singing;

and instantly the latch lifted, and a towering form strode across the threshold.

"Who was singing here?" said a voice from somewhere among the rafters.

Jacob's mother screamed—she understood Russian because she had served as cook in Odessa many years before her marriage; and the question suggested to her answers in the shape of knouts and prisons and Siberia, and fear tied her tongue.

"Who was singing here?" came the question more urgently.

The woman sprang up and threw herself on her knees before the intruder.

"Spare us, spare us, your honour," she stammered; "the boy did not know he was doing wrong. Did he disturb your honour in your sleep? or is it not lawful to sing the song?" And then she turned to her son and became fluent in chiding him. "Did I not tell thee, rascal, to let alone these songs of the Gentiles? Have I not begged of thee to sing the Synagogue tunes like 'He is the Tree of Life,' and 'There is none like him among the gods,' and such things, whereat none can take umbrage?—To be sure, your honour,

I have warned him, but he is obstinate and foolhardy: do not let your hand fall too heavy on us, for he is but a child without sense, and my husband served the Emperor loyally for twelve years."

The Cossack heard her patiently, then he smiled—at least Jacob saw his teeth gleam in the moonlight.

"My good woman," he said at last; "I have not come to harm you—there is nothing punishable in the boy's song, although it is the cause of my coming; but that is no business of yours. Come here, little throstle; who taught you that song?"

"What song, your honour?" whimpered Jacob, still very much frightened.

"The 'Minka, Minka' song."

And Jacob told him how there had come to the choir two years ago one Aaron, a tenor, and he it was who taught him the song. Aaron had learned it on his wanderings, somewhere in Livonia, and this same Aaron had afterwards gone to Warsaw and had there become a famous opera singer. Casimir nodded his head. Quite true, the song came from Livonia, for that he could vouch. That was where he had first heard it, and that was where he had met the Minka who had sung it to him in the drowsy summer afternoons, and had given the sunset a golden glory such as he had never seen before. And then, when his regiment had been ordered further, the memory of song and singer and sunset had followed him hauntingly, till he stretched out his arms in vain impotent longing for the dreamlike gladness of the past. Ever since he had seen no beauty in melody, nor in the smile of maidens, nor in the gorgeous phantasms of the summer sky. But at the sound of the selfsame song it was as though by a magic touch the old world were rising from its ruins; he was again lying on the heather with Minka beside him chasing the importunate gnats from his forehead, and singing with that soul-bewildering sweetness which only her happiness of heart could have taught her. And again he went through the short-lived period of Paradise—from the first mute comprehending look to the agonised bliss of the last embrace.

Jacob looked at him in wonder. What made the stern-faced man draw his lips together as if he were in pain? What put the far-away look into his eyes? Jacob would have pitied him, if there had been a man on the face of the earth bold enough to pity a Cossack.

Casimir took a chair and made himself at home.

"Will you sing that song again, little man?" he said.

Jacob was quite willing; he had lost all fear. The great big soldier spoke very kindly, almost pleadingly, so he began:

> "Minka, the plain is asleep,
> Minka, the moon——"

Casimir stopped him. "Wait a minute," he said, and got up to shut the open window. Jacob thought he looked jealous that anything of the tune should float away and be lost on the air.

Jacob began again, putting all his soul into his voice:

> "Minka, the plain is asleep,
> Minka, the moon is blind;
> Minka, the stars breathe deep—
> Their breath is the whispering wind."

And so it went on.

Casimir looked up with a sigh when it

was finished. "It does not seem so long ago, nor so far away after all," he muttered; and then, stroking Jacob's head, he said, "Good-night, little man; may the saints watch over you."

He went out very slowly, stopping to smile back from the door. The next evening he came again, and Jacob had to sing the "Minka" song once and twice and three times. Casimir tapped time with his foot, and tried to hum a bar or two under his breath in his bassoon gurgle; but it was not a success, for he sang dreadfully out of tune, and at last he gave it up and let Jacob sing on alone.

The third evening he came again. "I have brought you a present," he said; and out he fetched three big buttons of shining bronze, such as are worn on military uniforms, and a rusty spur. Jacob was delighted, especially with the bronze buttons, which were quite a treasure; for among his playmates they each counted equal in value to a whole dozen of the ordinary brass or bone article, and Jacob had been slightly out of luck in the button-game lately. As for the spur, it would sell for two copecks any hour in the day.

Henceforth Cossack and chorister were inseparable; wherever one was seen, the other was sure to be not many miles off. Jacob certainly neglected no opportunity of being about with his stalwart friend, and by force of example was gradually assuming a martial swagger that would have made him ludicrous in the eyes of his comrades if they had room for anything but jealousy at his glory.

It must be said, however, that there was nothing virulent in their envy. For the most part it resolved itself into a regretful self-pity; everybody cannot be so lucky as to have a real live Cossack for his bodyguard. The chief exception was Schmeyrel, the red-haired, pimple-faced fellow-chorister of Jacob. He also sang treble, but though he had an exceptionally good voice, it did not come up to Jacob's by a size and a half; and consequently it never fell to Schmeyrel's lot to sing the treble-solos wherever such occurred—a fact which he looked upon as a flagrant mistake in the dispensation of God's justice. He therefore did not love Jacob, and was not always complimentary in his criticisms of his favoured rival.

"Do you think he can sing?" he used to say; "if you throw your boots against the wall you will have more music than you could ever squeeze out of his voice."

And now when he saw the intimate relations between Jacob and Casimir, his bile was full to bursting. It only needed a sight of Jacob flying by on the Cossack's horse, with Casimir gripping him solicitously behind, to spoil Schmeyrel's appetite for the day; and as this sort of thing occurred at least once every twenty-four hours, he was in a fair way of dwindling down to a bag of bones. Thus desperate measures became necessary. Supplanting Jacob was impossible. Schmeyrel knew he sat too firm in the saddle of the Cossack's horse and the Cossack's affections. He therefore set about equalising matters by getting for himself a Cossack of his own.

How it was he smuggled himself into Sturak's good graces remained a mystery. His mother did not connect the event with the mysterious disappearance of the liver sausages and onion-strings from the hayloft, nor did his father associate it with the abnormally rapid decline of his brandy and tobacco. It was only when the roast goose, that was to have served for the Sabbath dinner, took wings unto itself and flew away that Schmeyrel's tactics of ingratiation fell under momentary suspicion. But he had attained his object; he was allowed to walk by Sturak's side, clutching him by the skirt of his coat; he could touch his lance, sit on his horse and avail himself of all the amenities of having a Cossack for an acquaintance. The one shadow of dissatisfaction consisted in the thought that herein also Jacob had outdistanced him: Jacob's Cossack was the Colonel's special orderly, whereas Sturak was only a mere rank-and-file man.

Strange to say, Sturak had himself remarked on this inequality of things, though not from Schmeyrel's point of view. He saw no reason why Casimir should be orderly and not he. There were privileges, perquisites, exemptions, connected with the post which made it desirable for having. Sturak had never failed to observe on the drill-ground how much more cool and comfortable Casimir must feel, sitting still on his horse, at a respectful distance behind the Colonel, than if he were engaged with the others in performing neck-breaking bewildering movements and evolutions, and choking all the time with dust and heat and vexation. He thought of Casimir's luck at the time when the elm forest outside the town had been struck by lightning and was blazing away merrily, so that Sturak and all his comrades had to turn out with axes to cut a clearing and prevent the fire causing further mischief. And what did Casimir do? Nothing; he just stood aside out of harm's way, superintending and giving directions, like a full-fledged non-commissioned officer, complacently watching the others getting scorched and blistered, not to mention the immediate possibility of their getting their heads broken by the down-crashing trunks. Oh, it was a grand thing to be the Colonel's orderly.

The summer had been quite young when the Cossacks came to Lotz; by the time it was middle-aged Casimir and Jacob seemed to have known each other all their lives. But much earlier in the day the confederacy had been raised to a trio. Satanas was a fine fellow, despite his congenital habit of going on four legs. His skin was smooth as velvet and black as jet, so that the whites of his eyes, shot with thin streaks of red, gleamed out in startling contrast. He was completed by an arching tail, which meant eternity to any presumptuous insect that came within the sweep and purchase of it. Casimir had cropped it by four inches, because otherwise Satanas flicked himself in the afore-mentioned eyes, which did not conduce to his good behaviour. For the maintenance of this Casimir was responsible. The horse belonged to the Colonel, and Casimir had his hands full in reminding this same Satanas that even the most high-spirited stallion has to conform to certain rules and restrictions not observed in his primitive state.

If any man could do that it was Casimir; he was noted as the best and boldest rough-rider within the range of the Uralo-Carpathians, and although Satanas came to him with the reputation of having kicked his mother and brother-foal to death, the mere sound of Casimir's voice soon began to have a most salutary effect on his morals. Occasionally the old, or rather the young Satanas peeped out of him, as in the case of the man who wagered he would ride him with spurs; that man never put on spurs again. Satanas soon saw that Jacob was a friend of his chamberlain, and under the circumstances found it expedient to treat him with a certain amount of consideration; and then he thought that this roundabout way was a waste of time, and determined to like the boy for his own sake.

So the three lived together in very good accord. Every afternoon Casimir took the horse to the river to give him his after-siesta bath; Jacob helped to rub him down, and in reward was allowed to ride him back to stable, with Casimir leading by the bridle. In the meantime the "Minka" song was not forgotten. Sometimes Casimir went about like a man in a trance, or stood looking northwards, his soul and body seemingly nothing but eyes. Jacob knew him in these moods; gently, as though it were merely the wind blowing in snatches of music, he started the song and gradually let it swell out in full sonorousness, till earth and sky seemed to be singing the glories of Minka. And in the end Casimir always came to himself with a little shiver, as though he had passed through a tense, soul-racking agony and felt he had still hope of life.

But once something very unpleasant occurred in connection with the song. It was a sultry night and the stars flashed as they flash only once in a thousand years, and Jacob had gone with Casimir to pass the night in the great barn that served as sleeping accommodation for the detachment. The others had all dozed off, but Casimir kept tossing and tossing from side to side on his truss; at last he sat up, and with his chin propped up on both hands gazed wearily at the heavens. Jacob watched him furtively for a while, and then crawling up to him put his arm round his friend's neck and whispered:

"Shall I sing it?"

Casimir nodded silently, and Jacob began in a low crooning tone which a nurse might use in soothing a fretful child. But it was not so soft but that the other sleepers should sleep through it, and one by one they lifted their heads and listened; perhaps it reminded them of their mothers and wives and sisters praying for them in their homes thousands and thousands of miles away.

But when Jacob had come as far as the middle, Sturak's voice came gruffly:

"What ails the Jew-brat? He whines like a wolf-cub that has fed on moonlight instead of mother's milk for a month. Silence, you whimpering cur."

Jacob looked up and saw Casimir signing to him to go on. That sufficed him; at Casimir's bidding he would have sung in defiance of all other Cossacks in the world.

"Silence, there," shouted Sturak again. "What, you will not? Then listen to this."

His foot shot out and Jacob flew forward as from a catapult, and the rest of the song tumbled out of him all at once in a heap of gasps and gurgles. Luckily Sturak's foot was unshod, else Jacob would not have been left with any backbone to speak of. Casimir got up very quietly, strode over to where Jacob lay, examined him and saw there was not much damage done. Relieved on that point, he went back into the barn and busied himself with Sturak; that is to say, with one hand he clutched him by his shoulder-strap and with the other by the belt, and banged him up and down on the straw pallet as if he were determined to get a bushel of grain out of the empty ears. Sturak protested, and if he had only once succeeded in getting his teeth firmly set in his assailant's wrist, the latter would have remembered it for many a day to come. But Casimir was lithe as an eel, and when he had done with Sturak as a threshing machine he threw him down with a decisive thud and went back to his couch. However, there was not much sleeping done in the barn that night; Casimir kept awake to prevent Sturak knifing him unawares, and the others had a disquieting notion that Sturak might fasten the barn door from outside and burn them as a sacrifice to his humiliated pride.

The report of the scrimmage got abroad, and Schmeyrel went about with mischievous insinuations concerning Jacob.

"Take care," he told everybody—"that vagabond will plunge us all into ruin; was it not through him that Sturak was nearly killed? And if it had not been for me and for my begging the Cossack with tears not to visit the sins of the guilty on the innocent, it would have gone hard with us; for he had sworn wherever he met a Jew to run him through the belly with his lance. But of course no one thanks me for what I do to the benefit of the congregation."

However, nothing more was heard of the affair, for Sturak thought there was always more to be lost than gained in trying tricks on Casimir. But he carefully made a note of the whole business and waited an opportunity when he could have his own say with safety. Jacob felt a little stiff for a few days, and then something of such moment happened as to put the recollection of his misadventure clean out of his mind.

The "magnum opus" of Myer Bachyah, the famous precentor of Lotz, was at last finished. Twelve months had he been about his setting of the passage "The Lord is King," that is said during the Friday Evening Service, and in all he had made five different and distinct draughts of the composition before he was satisfied with his work. And a wonderful thing it was—so much could be seen even from the imperfect renderings of the initial rehearsals. It started by being chanted right through as a solo by each of the four part-voices, and the accompaniment of the other three was varied in every case. This served as an introduction, and then it was gone through twice in a grand *ensemble*—the first time in "dur" the second in "moll." Then the precentor himself declaimed it as a recitative, and after that came the item *de resistance*—a treble monologue sung by one voice, for which, of course, Jacob had been cast from the start. The subsequent and diversified movements of "The Lord is King" are too numerous to specify—how numerous may be gauged by intimation being sent to the Wardens of the Synagogue that on the eve of its production they had better provide candles three times the length of those used on less conspicuous occasions. Yes, "The Lord is King" was undoubtedly a great work, with fugues and coloratures of the most neck-twisting descriptions, with startling paradoxes of counterpoint and contra C's for the basses and top C's for the tenors in wasteful profusion. There was not a chorister in Bachya's choir who did not pat himself on the back for having cast in his lot with so distinguished a precentor. Their fame was now assured, for the work would take its triumphant course through all the synagogues of Poland, Slavonia, Kurland, into Hungary and Austria, and they, the original interpreters, would live long in the memories and traditions of their imitators. The solo-singers—all except little Jacob, the greatest of them—gave themselves high airs and swelled visibly with conceit and a sense of indispensability.

Bachya was very pleased with the progress of the rehearsals, and announced that the *début* of "The Lord is King" was fixed for the eve of the Sabbath of Repentance, which would invest it with greater *éclat*, this being the most momentous of all Sabbaths because it is the immediate forerunner of the Day of Atonement; and, despite the stress of their own duties, the precentors of Linschitz, Klom, Volesen, and all the neighbouring towns had promised to grace the occasion with their presence. And as the decisive day drew near and things were getting shipshape, Bachya and his choristers went about with the exhilarating consciousness of having a sensation in store for the world.

Jacob had not seen so much of Casimir lately, but for all that there was no slackening of their friendship. The only difference was that as time went on a change came over the Cossack's disposition which Jacob could not fathom. There was a restlessness, an anxious expectancy about him, as though the future were big with tremendous consequences. But when Jacob met him on the morning of the great "The Lord is King" Friday, the look he saw on Casimir's face almost made him cry out in wonder; the man seemed transfigured.

"What has happened?" he asked. "Why, Casimir, you look as if you had been born all over again."

Casimir smiled. "Don't ask questions, little man," he said, "you don't understand these things." And then he sank his voice to a conspirator's whisper. "Do you know what I am going to do? I am going away the whole day; the Colonel is out wolf-hunting, and he won't know. Come with me—I must find some one to give Satanas his afternoon splash; it is getting cold, and there won't be many more for him this season."

Jacob trotted along merrily. "Shall I go down to the river with him?" he asked.

"If you like—why not?" was the answer.

"And may I ride him back?"

Casimir looked serious. "I don't know," he said at last; "it is rather risky without me."

"But he knows me by now," protested Jacob; "he pricks up his ears when he hears me coming and neighs. I think he likes me as well as you."

"Hm," observed Casimir, cautiously. He knew that Satanas' affection for him was tempered to a certain extent with fear. But there was nothing to be afraid of in little Jacob, and therefore the animal's liking for him was perhaps of a more genuine sort, which made things more hopeful as far as Jacob's request was concerned.

"Well, if you will be very careful," was the decision; "sit very still and don't let the reins flap, else he might think some one was flogging him."

Jacob promised faithfully to keep a zealous guard over his neck and legs, for the normal condition of which he had a strong partiality. Then they went and found a beetle-browed, heavy-jawed Wallachian who undertook to act as Casimir's substitute.

The whole forenoon Jacob lounged aimlessly about the streets, the more at a loss for diversion because the afternoon and evening were to be a programme of incidents; besides he was rather impatient to try how much influence he individually possessed over Satanas. He was therefore in good time at the stables, and superintended the removal of Satanas with the air of a proprietor. The river passed by the outskirts of the town, and soon the whole cavalcade of men and horses was sleepily wending its way thither through the sultry afternoon. Jacob passed Schmeyrel walking at Sturak's side.

"Have you been sucking raw eggs?" shouted Schmeyrel.

"What for?" asked Jacob, off his guard.

"To make your voice a bit smoother; it rasps like a grater."

Schmeyrel knew he was telling a lie, and Jacob knew of Schmeyrel's knowledge, and therefore did not trouble to continue the topic, reserving his demonstration for the evening.

In a little while the whole troop were plunging and spuming in the freshening waters, that sucked the seething heat-fever out of their veins. Satanas was behaving in best style; of course he was aware that Casimir was away, but the presence of Jacob was a guarantee that things were as they should be. So when after the ablutions Jacob mounted him, it was only what he expected.

The others were cantering on in front; Satanas was right behind, for Jacob was mindful of Casimir's precept to use him gently; the Wallachian walked stolidly by his side, one hand on the bridle. Gradually one of the other mounts fell back, and Jacob saw it was Sturak with Schmeyrel on the saddle in front of him. Schmeyrel had cut himself a withe from the bank, and was swishing it in the air. The two horses trotted side by side with a fair distance between them. Then Sturak edged up closer, keeping somewhat in the rear, so that Jacob hardly noticed that they were only an arm's length or so apart.

Sturak was eyeing Satanas with sidelong glances, and somehow the beast gave to him a suggestion of which he had long been in search. If Schmeyrel should chance to whip him ever so lightly with his withe there would probably be consequences not redounding to Casimir's credit in his capacity of Colonel's orderly; it would also incidentally wipe off the little score still due to him from the barn episode.

"Strike him," he whispered in Schmeyrel's ear.

Schmeyrel did not at once catch the drift of the bidding. Then it came home to him that if he sent Satanas tearing away with his rider there would, in all likelihood, not be sufficient of the rider left to sing the treble solo in "The Lord is King" that evening. And of course there would be requisition of himself as understudy. With a deft insidious movement he lashed Satanas across the haunches. Satanas walked on unconcernedly; he felt the sting, but then he thought there must be a mistake somewhere; no one would take such a liberty with him.

Sturak could not make it out. "Strike harder," he whispered again, and Schmeyrel struck harder.

This time Satanas was certain, and did

not stay to see if the arm of the Wallachian was still in its socket or if he had pulled it out by the roots. With a shrill whistle of anger he levelled his neck and leapt forward as if there were myriads of hornets and gadflies behind him. Jacob had just time to throw himself flat and clutch as much of the coal-black mane as his convulsive little hands could hold. And then he lay quite still, sucking himself on to the maddened brute with all the pores of his body. So he flew on, passing the straggling groups ahead one by one. In wonder and terror they stared after the hapless rider, but no one stirred a finger; it would be madness to get in the way of that stampeding avalanche of hoof and tail and foam. Jacob felt nothing, only the hissing, whizzing noise in his ears, and the black dancing spots that kept circling before his eyes. His limbs were numbed with a narcotic torpor, and he breathed only when the vice across his chest grew so tight that it seemed gripping his life by the very core. Where were they taking him too? Perhaps to his father in heaven; well, then, he hoped he would get there soon, for he was quite tired of the deserts and deserts of nothingness he had already traversed. At one place he heard a loud shriek which he knew was his mother's, and from that he gathered he must be somewhere near the synagogue, for she had gone betimes to get a good seat from which to feast her eyes and ears on the one lamb that made all her flock.

For all we know this might have been the last of Satanas and Jacob. But that would be forgetting the existence of Casimir and the special providence that watched over "The Lord is King" cantata. Casimir had done his day's business, and was walking home very pleased with himself and everybody else. Just as he was turning the cross-road he caught the sound of trampling. "A runaway horse," he said to himself; he ought to have known, for runaway horses were a speciality of his. On a nearer view he found the horse was black, was running as if it had split its four legs into eight, and consequently was Satanas; there was a moveless little figure clinging to his neck, with its yellow curls fluttering in the wind like a flag, and which presumably was Jacob: the situation was quite clear.

Casimir knew better than to fling his arms about like a windmill and halloo; Satanas was going quite fast enough without giving him reasonable motive for an extra spurt. So he waited till they were abreast, and then proceeded to test how far he could stretch his legs without actually dislocating them. Man and beast ran on side by side till they had come to a spread of green turf, and then Casimir saw his chance. Bending forward he just whispered one word, "Satanas!" and Satanas stood still as if his feet had suddenly grown into the earth. But Casimir ran full two yards forward, opened his arms and dexterously caught the limp, huddled form which he knew would come whirling through the air with a semi-circular sweep.

Five minutes afterwards Jacob was saying, "Is that you, Casimir?"

"Yes, little man"—there was half a sob in the answer.

"Casimir."

"What, Jacob?"

"Tell me the truth—am I alive?"

Casimir would have laughed, but he lacked the requisite breath.

"Yes, Jacob, you are alive," he said, soberly.

"Then come and let me tell my mother so."

He suddenly grasped what had been the nagging thought at the back of his brain that had kept him from dying.

"The Lord is King" was a portentous success—there were no two opinions about it. Casimir, who had been standing open-mouthed all through, thought that Jacob had sung more gloriously than he had ever sung the "Minka" song; but perhaps Jacob's rendering had lost some of its merit in consequence of certain events.

The following Sunday Jacob met Casimir coming out of church, but he was not alone; there was a young woman with him, by her dress evidently a Livonian. Jacob turned tail to run, but Casimir caught him gently by the arm and said smilingly:

"Jacob, this is Minka; was she not worth while singing of?"

THE END.

www.ingramcontent.com/pod-product-compliance
Lightning Source LLC
Chambersburg PA
CBHW022101230426
43672CB00008B/1243